LONDON ESCAPES

Over 70 Captivating Day Trips from London

David Hampshire

T0163124

City Books • Bath • England

First published 2019

Copyright © City Books 2019
Cover Photo: Brighton (Adobe Stock)
Cover Design: Herring Bone Design

City Books, c/o Survival Books Limited
Office 169, 3 Edgar Buildings
George Street, Bath BA1 2FJ, United Kingdom
+44 (0)1305-266918, info@survivalbooks.net
citybooks.co, survivalbooks.net and londons-secrets.com

British Library Cataloging in Publication Data
A CIP record for this book is available
from the British Library.
ISBN: 978-1-913171-00-1

Printed in India
Production managed by Jellyfish Print Solutions

Acknowledgements

The author would like to thank the many people who helped with research and provided information for this book. Special thanks are due to Gwen Simmonds and Richard Todd for their invaluable research, Robbi Atilgan for editing; Susan Griffith for final proof checking; John Marshall for desktop publishing and photo selection; David Gillingwater for cover design; Jim Watson for the maps; and the author's wife for the constant supply of tea and coffee. Last, but not least, a special thank you to the many photographers – the unsung heroes – whose beautiful images bring the destinations to life.

The Author

David Hampshire's career has taken him around the world and he lived and worked in many countries before taking up writing full-time. He's the author, co-author or editor of over 30 titles, including *London's Secret Places, London's Secrets: Museums & Galleries, London's Secrets: Parks & Gardens, London's Green Walks, London's Village Walks, London's Monumental Walks* and *Peaceful London*. David was born in Surrey and lived and worked in London for many years and still considers himself a Londoner. Nowadays he divides his time between London and Dorchester (Dorset).

The Publisher

City Books is an imprint of Survival Books, which was established in 1987 and by the mid-1990s was the leading publisher of books for expats and migrants planning to live, work, buy property or retire abroad. In 2000, we published the first of our London books, *Living and Working in London*, and since then have published over 20 additional London titles, including a series of city walking guides. We now specialise in alternative London guidebooks for both residents and visitors. See our websites for our latest titles.

Readers' Guide

◆ **Contact details:** These include the address, postcode and website. You can enter the postcode to display a map of the location on Google and other map sites or, if you're driving, enter the postcode on your satnav.

◆ **Rail:** Train times are from the Trainline website (thetrainline.com) and may vary depending on the time of day and day of the week. Most venues are served by direct trains – when a change is necessary it's indicated – but may involve a further bus or taxi journey or a 'short' walk.

◆ **Road:** Approximate travel times by road from central London are taken from the AA Route Planner (theaa.com/route-planner/index.jsp) and vary considerably depending on traffic and weather conditions. Note that parking is difficult (and expensive) in some towns and cities and not all venues provide free parking.

◆ **Opening Times:** These may vary depending on the time of year, particularly during public holiday periods, and the day of the week. Some venues are open only in spring/summer. Check websites for current times.

◆ **Fees:** Where applicable, entrance fees (2019) for an adult/child (under 5s are usually free) are shown and don't include extras such as Gift Aid. Some venues offer concessions for families, students and pensioners. You may receive a reduction if you book online – and can also avoid ticket queues – and/or travel by public transport (tickets must be produced). When entry to a venue is free, it's indicated.

◆ **Nearby:** Interesting places nearby are listed – those featured in this book are shown in **bold**.

◆ **Food & Drink:** Recommended cafés, pubs and restaurants are included for all venues. Telephone numbers are listed where bookings are advisable or necessary, otherwise booking isn't usually required or even possible. A rough price guide is included – £ = inexpensive, ££ = moderate – most places fall into the inexpensive category.

Contents

Disabled Access

Many historic public and private buildings don't provide wheelchair access or provide wheelchair access to the ground floor only. Wheelchairs are provided at some venues (although users may need assistance) and you may also be able to hire a mobility 'scooter'. Most museums, galleries and public buildings have a WC, although it may not be wheelchair accessible. Contact venues directly if you have specific requirements. The Disabled Go website (disabledgo.com) provides more in-depth access information for some destinations.

King's College Chapel, Cambridge (see page 17)

Introduction

Samuel Johnson famously observed that 'when a man is tired of London, he is tired of life' and no one would deny that the city is an exciting and stimulating place to live and visit, offering a wealth of diversions. However, even old Sam would no doubt agree that sometimes you need a change of scenery – to escape the city's constant hustle and bustle and visit somewhere quieter with a gentler, slower pace of life. London is also the perfect base for vistors wishing to explore southeast England's numerous attractions.

When you yearn for some bracing sea air or wish to commune with nature, experience life in an idyllic village or imagine you're lord of the manor, get up close and personal with some exotic wildlife or treat the kids to an exhilarating day out, *London Escapes* will point you in the right direction. It contains over 70 great day trips – from historical towns and charming villages to magnificent stately homes and gardens, nostalgic seaside resorts and lovely beaches to spectacular parks and nature reserves – with something to suit every taste.

A plethora of tour operators offer coach trips to major attractions from London – including many of the destinations featured in this book – or you can travel by private car. However, we believe in letting the 'train take the strain', which is the most relaxing and often the fastest way to travel (strikes excepted!). All the places highlighted can be reached in under two hours by train (or car) and many in under an hour – usually by direct trains. Travelling by car generally takes longer and you also have the problem and added expense of parking. However, some destinations, particularly those without a direct rail link from London, are easier to reach by car (and one – Woburn Safari Park – is accessible only by car), which also allows you to tour an area and visit nearby attractions at the same time.

A good day out deserves a good lunch and *London Escapes* contains recommendations – historic pubs, relaxing restaurants and cosy cafés – where you can be assured of a tasty meal. Many venues – such as stately homes, gardens and theme parks – have on-site cafés/restaurants and provide dedicated picnic areas.

So, why not escape the city for a day and explore the exciting world of adventures on London's doorstep? We trust you'll enjoy discovering them as much as we did.

David Hampshire
July 2019

GLOUCESTERSHIRE

OXFORDSHIRE

Chilterns

Legoland

Cookham

BERKSHIRE

Windsor

Highclere Castle

Thorpe Park

Bath

RHS
Wisley

WILTSHIRE

Painshill Park

The Sculpture Park

Shere

Watts Gallery &
Artists' Village

Polesden
Lacey

SOMERSET

Stonehenge

HAMPSHIRE

SURREY

Salisbury

Winchester

Petwor

WEST SUSS

Bosham

Worth

DORSET

Beaulieu

Chichester

ISLE OF
WIGHT

South of London

ESSEX

GREATER LONDON

Chilterns

RAF Museum

Elmley National
Nature Reserve

Claremont
Landscape
Garden

Chistlehurst
Caves

Margate

or

Rochester

Whitstable

Ramsgate

Park

Chessington World
of Adventures

Faversham

RHS
Wisley

Canterbury

Deal

Shere

Knole House

Leeds Castle

Chilham

Mayfield
Lavender Farm

Chartwell

KENT

Polesden
Lacey

Dorking & Surrey Hills

Chiddingstone

Sissinghurst
Castle Garden

SURREY

Bluebell
Railway

Port Lympne

Leonardslee
Gardens

Rye

EAST SUSSEX

Petworth House

WEST SUSSEX

Ridgeway Vineyard

Hastings

ichester

Worthing

Brighton

Alfriston

Eastbourne

● Towns & Cities	● Parks, Gardens & Nature Reserves
● Villages	● Mainly for Kids
● Coastal Resorts	● Miscellaneous
● Stately Homes	

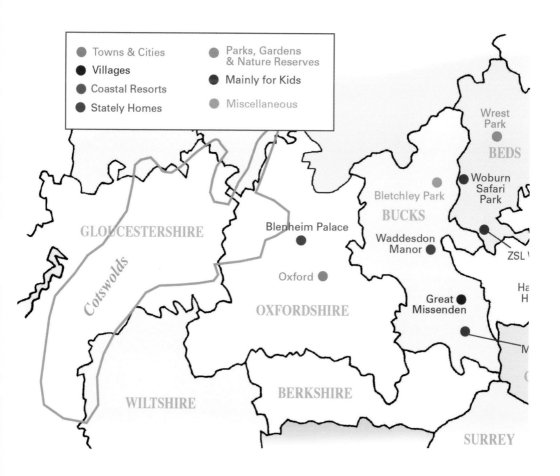

Legend:
- Towns & Cities
- Villages
- Coastal Resorts
- Stately Homes
- Parks, Gardens & Nature Reserves
- Mainly for Kids
- Miscellaneous

GLOUCESTERSHIRE

Cotswolds

BLENHEIM PALACE

Oxford

OXFORDSHIRE

WILTSHIRE

BERKSHIRE

Wrest Park

BEDS

Bletchley Park

BUCKS

Woburn Safari Park

Waddesdon Manor

ZSL W

Ha
H

Great Missenden

M

SURREY

North of London

Cambridge

Lavenham

East
Bergholt

Saffron Walden

HERTS

Knebworth
House

Coggeshall

Colchester

ESSEX

ZSL Whipsnade Zoo

Mersea Island

St Albans

Hatfield
House

Epping
Forest

Bekonscot
Model Village

Leigh-on-Sea

GREATER LONDON

Rainham
Marshes

KENT

EDS

Salisbury Cathedral, Wiltshire (see page 47)

1.
Towns & Cities

Scores of cities and towns are accessible from London for day trips. We have chosen fourteen of the most interesting and rewarding, which are less that 90 minutes by train (usually more by car). These include the beautiful UNESCO World Heritage city of Bath; the historic university cities of Cambridge and Oxford; the ancient cathedral cities of Canterbury, St Albans and Winchester; plus less well-known (but no less interesting) small towns which include Faversham, Saffron Walden and Rye.

Before setting out it's worth doing some research to decide what you most want to see (useful websites are listed), as it's often impossible to see everything on a day trip, particularly when visiting the larger cities. Nearby places of interest that can be visited on a day trip are also shown.

Bath

Address: Bath BA1 5AW (visitbath.co.uk)

Rail: from 1h 30min via Paddington station

Road: 2h 20min (115mi) via M4

Nearby: Bradford-on-Avon, Castle Combe, **Cotswolds**, Dyrham Park

Set in the rolling countryside of the River Avon valley, beautiful Bath – the only city in the UK that's designated a UNESCO World Heritage Site (since 1987) – is located in Somerset, 115 miles west of London and 11 miles southeast of Bristol. Famous for its natural hot springs and ravishing Georgian architecture – built from local honey-coloured Bath stone – a stroll around Bath is a journey through centuries of architectural delights. These include splendid 16th-century **Bath Abbey** (fee), noted for its fan-vaulting, tower (which you can climb) and striking stained-glass windows; the majestic **Royal Crescent** and inspired **Circus**; along with a wealth of gorgeous streets and buildings. Don't miss the

Assembly Rooms (free), the social hub of Georgian Bath, or the chance to stroll along Great Pulteney Street and across **Pulteney Bridge**, inspired by Florence's Ponte Vecchio and one of only four bridges in the world lined with shops.

Pulteney Bridge

Built for pleasure and relaxation – it was the centre of fashionable life in England during the 18th century – Bath has been a spa destination since Roman times. The waters remain a big draw, both the ancient **Roman Baths** (*Aquae Sulis*) and the modern **Thermae Bath Spa** (see box), the only natural thermal hot springs in Britain where you can still wallow in the waters. Restored in 2011, the Roman-era baths are now a museum (fee) and include the Great Bath, Roman statues and a temple, comprising one of the finest historic sites in Northern Europe. The city's unique thermal springs rise here and the Baths still flow with natural hot water, while interactive exhibits and computer-generated reconstructions illustrate their importance to our Roman ancestors.

Bath has a wide choice of museums and galleries, and enjoys year-round festivals, theatre, music and sports. If it's culture you're after, there's an abundance of choice, including the impressive **Holburne Museum**

Roman Baths

Parade Gardens

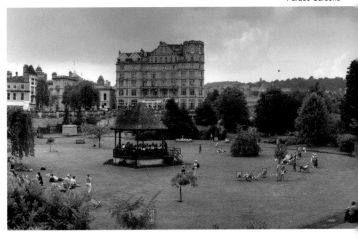

(home to the fascinating collection of Sir William Holburne); the **Fashion Museum** (fee) at the Bath Assembly Rooms; the museum of Georgian life at **No 1 Royal Crescent** (fee); classic and contemporary art at the splendid **Victorian Art Gallery** (free); Bath's **Old Theatre Royal**, opened in 1750, home to the excellent **Masonic Museum** (fee); and the **Jane Austen Centre** (fee), which celebrates one of Britain's favourite authors, who lived in Bath 1801-06. A short way out of town is the **American Museum** (fee), set within 125 acres of beautiful grounds, home to the finest collection of Americana outside the United

States. Bath also offers an abundance of commercial art galleries and antiques shops.

If you wish to stretch your legs, Bath has some beautiful parks and gardens, including the expansive **Royal Victoria Park** (57 acres) and **Botanical Gardens**, the bijou riverside **Parade Gardens** (fee), charming **Henrietta Park** and delightful **Sydney Gardens** straddling the Kennet & Avon Canal. A short walk from the centre, **Alexandra Park** offers spectacular views

Thermae Bath Spa

Although you can no longer take the waters at the Roman Baths, you can enjoy the same natural hot spring water at the award-winning Thermae Bath Spa, which brings the spa into the 21st century, with luxurious treatments and a rooftop pool offering panoramic views over the city (thermaebathspa.com).

Royal Crescent

over the city, while a bit further away is magnificent **Prior Park** (National Trust, fee), an 18th-century landscape garden created by Bath entrepreneur Ralph Allen (1693-1764).

Holburne Museum

When you need a break from sight-seeing, the city is overflowing with places to eat and drink, and also offers some of the best independent shops and boutiques in the UK, along with the indoor Guildhall Market, a weekly farmers' market, and regular antiques fairs and markets. If you're tempted to remain longer you'll find a profusion of excellent hotels, fine dining and no less than five theatres. The annual programme of festivals includes the Bath Festival (music and literature) in May and the Jane Austen Festival in September.

Food & Drink

• **Circus Restaurant:** Located on Brock Street between the Circus and Royal Crescent, the award-winning Circus Restaurant serves modern British cuisine and is an excellent choice for a tasty lunch (01225-466020, lunch noon-2.30pm, 2pm Sat, closed Sun, £-££).

• **Sotto Sotto:** Popular Italian restaurant and bar located in atmospheric, 18th-century barrel vaults just south of Parade Gardens, Sotto offers classic Italian cuisine (01225-330236, noon-2pm, 5-10pm, £).

• **Pump Room Restaurant:** An elegant restaurant housed in the splendid Georgian Pump Room on Stall Street, one of the city's most historic lunch venues and a perfect setting for afternoon tea (01225-444477, lunch noon-2pm, afternoon tea noon-4.30pm, ££).

Bath Panorama

Cambridge

Address: Cambridge CB1 0AP (visitcambridge.org)

Rail: from 48min via King's Cross, St Pancras and Liverpool Street stations

Road: 1h 40min (65mi) via M11

Nearby: Bury St Edmunds, Ely, Newmarket, **Saffron Walden**

River Cam at Jesus Green

The county town of Cambridgeshire, Cambridge lies on the River Cam 65 miles north of London, just south of the low-lying coastal wetland known as the Fens. An important trading centre during the Roman and Viking periods, the first town charters were granted in the 12th century, although modern city status wasn't officially conferred until 1951. Quintessentially English (possibly the most English of all English cities), with its rich history, charming streets, stunning architecture, bucolic riverside walks, lovely open parkland, handsome pubs and much more, Cambridge is difficult to beat for a day trip from London.

The city is synonymous with its world-class university (cam.ac.uk) founded in 1209, although the oldest existing college, Peterhouse, wasn't established until 1284. It has much in common with Oxford University (see page 34) – from ancient colleges to a shared affection for the flat-bottomed pleasure boats known as punts – but has more green space, less traffic and is much prettier than its academic rival.

A tour of the majestic university colleges is a must and the highlight of any visit. There are 31 colleges – founded between the 13th and 20th centuries – each with its own separate grounds and gardens, student

King's College

Bridge of Sighs, St John's College

St Mary the Great

north end of King's Parade. Built in the 15th century – a parish church and the university church of Cambridge University – it has a fine interior and a tower dating from 1608. Also of note is **Little St Mary's Church** (St Mary the Less, 1352), which is noted for its beautiful stained-glass windows, and the **Round Church** (aka the Church of the Holy Sepulchre), built around 1130 and one of only four Norman round churches in England. Other historic churches worth a visit include St Bene't's (c 1020) – the oldest building in Cambridge – St Clement's (1225) and St Botolph's (c 1350).

housing, chapels, dining halls and classrooms. A visit to any college is worthwhile, but the most popular include King's College (and its magnificent chapel), Trinity College (home of Sir Christopher Wren's Library), Peterhouse, St John's – famous for its romantic Bridge of Sighs – and Queen's College. The latter features the wooden Mathematical Bridge, so called because it was built without nails, relying for its strength on meticulous calculation (although today's version is a 1902 reconstruction).

Cambridge also has a treasure trove of beautiful medieval churches, which include the **Church of St Mary the Great**, aka Great St Mary's or GSM, at the

Kettle's Yard

Cambridge offers something for everyone when it comes to culture and entertainment, including a variety of museums and galleries, an exciting theatre and performance scene encompassing drama, dance and family entertainment, and a wide range of music from

---

College Visitor Information & Fees

For college opening times and fees (if applicable), see cambridge-news.co.uk/news/cambridge-news/cambridge-university-colleges-free-visit-13810784.

Fitzwilliam Museum

pop to classical, jazz to rap, not forgetting the sublime choir of King's College Chapel.

The city's many museums – eight cultural and scientific museums are operated by Cambridge University alone – include the splendid **Fitzwilliam Museum** (free), whose world-class collections of art and antiquities span centuries and include masterpieces by Titian, Modigliani and Picasso, along with ancient artefacts from Egypt, Greece and Rome. Another must-see collection is **Kettle's Yard** (free), the former home of one-time Tate curator Jim Ede, housing a major collection of 20th-century and contemporary art, including works by Ben Nicholson, Barbara Hepworth, Henry Moore, Joan Miró and Constantin Brancusi.

> When you've had your fill of academia, a punting trip along the River Cam is a splendid way to see the city on a summer's day, perhaps culminating in a picnic alongside the Backs, the meadows bordering the willow-shaded Cam.

Other museums include the Museum of Cambridge, the Museum of Archaeology & Anthropology, the Museum of Classical Archaeology, the Sedgwick Museum of Earth Sciences, the Polar Museum, the University Museum of Zoology, the Whipple Museum

Punts on River Cam

Botanical Garden

of the History of Science, the Cambridge Museum of Technology, and the Centre for Computing History.

If you fancy a walk (or bike ride) after all that culture, Cambridge offers an abundance of green spaces, including magnificent riverside parks, tranquil water meadows and ravishing gardens. The natural fen landscape flows gently through the city centre along the **River Cam**, with cows grazing within sight of glorious **King's College Chapel**, and the beautifully manicured college grounds, fellows' gardens and the university's lovely **Botanic Garden** (fee) dating from 1831. The city's public parks and commons are a paradise for children and include **Jesus Green** (close to Jesus College), where the river laps its northern edge and an avenue of London plane trees provides a leafy canopy, while adjoining

Christ's Pieces

Food & Drink

- **Cambridge Chop House:** Popular restaurant just 50m from King's College Chapel, with a traditional, British vibe and an emphasis on meat (01223-359506, lunch daily from noon, £-££).

- **The Eagle:** This huge 17th-century Greene King pub in Bene't Street – the venue where the discovery of DNA was announced in 1953 – is a good spot for a traditional pub lunch (01223-505020, 11am-11pm, midnight Thu-Sat, £).

- **The Senate:** Cheery bar and bistro with an all-day Mediterranean menu of tasty dishes, alongside champagne and cocktails (01223-315641, Mon-Thu 11.30am-10pm, Fri-Sat 9am-10pm, Sun 10am-6pm, £).

Midsummer Common is an ancient area of grassland bordered by the Cam, where you can watch the rowers on the water. In the city centre to the east of Christ's College is **Christ's Pieces**, a splendid Victorian park with ornamental trees and flower beds, while a short distance away is **Parker's Piece**, a 25-acre common regarded as the birthplace of the rules of association football (soccer).

When you're peckish or fancy a drink, Cambridge offers something for every palate, from Michelin-star cuisine (it's a gourmet's paradise) to fast food. It's noted for its pubs, from traditional to trendy, city or river views, tasty pub grub to gastro fare, along with a wide range of real ales. If you fancy a longer stay – and who wouldn't – Cambridge offers a plethora of inviting places to lay your head, enough shops to satisfy the most ardent shopaholic, and a range of theatres and music venues to while away the evening.

It's impossible to see all Cambridge has to offer on a day trip – but at less than an hour from London by train, it's easy to return!

Newnham College

Mathematical Bridge, Queen's College

Canterbury

Address: Canterbury, Kent CT1 1YW (canterbury.co.uk)

Rail: from 51min via St Pancras International, Charing Cross and Cannon Street stations

Road: 1h 30min (61mi) via M2 and A2

Nearby: Chilham, **Faversham**, Isle of Thanet, **Whitstable**

Christ Church Gate

One of England's most attractive and important cathedral cities, Canterbury in east Kent is 61 miles from London astride the River Stour. The area has been inhabited since prehistoric times and was the capital of the Celtic Cantiaci and the Jute Kingdom of Kent. In the 1st century AD it was captured by the Romans and named *Durovernum Cantiacorum*. Today, Canterbury is a beautiful city whose charming alleyways and lanes still follow the medieval street plan, with the River Stour meandering through its centre. It's a city where it's a pleasure to wander aimlessly, with something to delight around every corner, and street names – from Butchery Lane to Iron Bar Lane – reflect their original purpose. A boat trip on the Stour (aka Great Stour) is also highly recommended.

Canterbury Cathedral (fee) is a gem – a UNESCO World Heritage Site since 1988 – and the centre of English Christianity since St Augustine, its first bishop, converted the Saxons here in 597. You enter the cathedral precinct via the monumental **Christ Church Gate**, built to celebrate the marriage of Arthur, Prince of Wales, to Catherine of Aragon in 1502; unfortunately Arthur died a few months later and the gate wasn't finished for another 20 years. Vast, beautiful and inspiring, the cathedral has a history that's intrinsically linked

Canterbury Cathedral

St Augustine's Abbey

Canterbury isn't noted for its museums and galleries, although it has a number of important collections, including the fascinating **Beaney House of Art and Knowledge** (free), the city's central museum, library and art gallery, housed in a handsome Tudor Revival building. A little further along the High Street (next to the river) is **Eastbridge Hospital** (fee), aka the Hospital of St Thomas the Martyr – not a hospital as we know it today but a place of hospitality for pilgrims visiting Becket's shrine for over 800 years – an atmospheric building dating from 1190, with Gothic archways and a

to that of England. It's the seat of the Archbishop of Canterbury, leader of the Church of England, and the most important Christian site in the country.

After you've explored the cathedral and its cloisters and gardens, you can visit the ruins of 6th-century **St Augustine's Abbey** (fee) just outside the city walls, where St Augustine and King Ethelbert (550-616) are buried. Also worth a look is **St Martin's Church** (a short walk from St Augustine's), the first and oldest church in England, recognised along with the cathedral and abbey as part of the World Heritage Site. St Martin's was founded as the private chapel of Queen Bertha of Kent in the 6th century before Augustine arrived from Rome.

Eastbridge Hospital

St Martin's Church

Thomas Becket

Canterbury Cathedral is infamous as the place where Archbishop Thomas Becket was murdered in 1170, an event memorialised in TS Eliot's *Murder in the Cathedral*, which was premiered at the cathedral. A journey of pilgrims to Becket's shrine served as the basis of Geoffrey Chaucer's 14th-century classic, *The Canterbury Tales*, which you can discover more about at the **Canterbury Tales Visitor Attraction** (fee) in St Margaret's Street.

Marlow Theatre

The Marlowe Theatre is named in honour of local hero Christopher Marlowe (1564-1593), playwright and poet who hailed from Canterbury. Marlowe was a contemporary of Shakespeare, who was born in the same year.

international importance. The **Westgate**, built in 1380 and England's largest surviving medieval gateway, houses an interesting museum in its towers and offers spectacular views from its battlements.

The Old Weavers House

13th-century mural. There's also a small **Roman Museum** (fee) containing the remains of a wonderful Roman villa and its beautifully preserved mosaic floors, augmented with clever computer reconstructions and time tunnels. Plus the **Kent Museum of Freemasonry** (free) boasts a rare collection of national and

The city isn't well endowed with parks and gardens, although the pretty **Westgate Gardens** are well worth a stroll, with the River Stour and Westgate as a backdrop to the beautiful flowerbeds and majestic trees. Along the other leg of the Stour are **Greyfriars** (aka Franciscan) **Gardens**, a haven of peace in the heart of the city (owned by Eastbridge Hospital – see above). It's also the site of **Greyfriars Chapel**, the only remaining building of the first English Franciscan Friary built in 1267. To the south of the city is **Dane John Gardens**, a tranquil historic park containing a 1st-century AD burial mound, located within the city walls and dating back to 1551. Just east of here are the ruins of **Canterbury Castle**, one of the three original royal castles of Kent (the

Westgate Gardens

Food & Drink

- **Corner House**: Fine dining restaurant in a 16th-century former coach house overlooking the city walls, serving British produce (01227-780793, lunch noon-2.30pm, Sat noon-9.30pm, Sun noon-3.30pm, £-££).

- **Goods Shed Restaurant:** Excellent restaurant that's part of the Goods Shed food emporium, housed in a handsome former Regency railway depot (01227-459153, Tue-Fri 8am-11pm, Sat 9am-11pm, Sun 9.30am-4pm, £-££).

- **Pork & Co:** Popular fast food outlet on Sun Street, noted for its pulled pork but also offering a range of beef and chicken dishes. Carnivore heaven! (Mon-Sat 11am-9pm, Sun 11am-8pm, £).

fine restaurants offering a wide choice of cuisines, while foodies will love the Goods Shed, a daily farmers' market with an excellent on-site restaurant (see **Food & Drink**). If you have any time left before your train leaves, why not spend it exploring the city's meandering alleyways (again) and perhaps indulge in a little retail therapy.

others are Rochester Castle and Dover Castle), built soon after the Battle of Hastings in 1066 to mark the route taken by William the Conqueror to London.

Canterbury has a variety of venues for music, comedy and drama, including two theatres, the Marlowe Theatre (see box) and the Gulbenkian, home to a theatre, cinema and café. The cathedral, too, hosts musical and theatrical events – from choral performances and recitals to tea dances – and the Canterbury Festival, which takes place in and around the city every autumn, includes music, art, comedy, circus, theatre, walks, talks and more. When you've worked up an appetite, you'll find an abundance of superb historic pubs and a host of

Butchery Lane

Chichester

> **Address:** Chichester, West Sussex PO19 1LQ
> (visitchichester.org)
>
> **Rail:** from 1h 28min via London Bridge and
> London Victoria stations
>
> **Road:** 1h 50min (81mi) via A3
>
> **Nearby:** Arundel, **Bosham**, Bognor Regis,
> Goodwood, **Petworth House**

Situated on the River Lavant, 81 miles southwest of London, Chichester is the county town of West Sussex; in fact, it's the county's only city, despite having a population of less than 30,000. It has a long history as a Roman settlement (when it was called *Noviomagus Reginorum*) and was an important town in Saxon times. The plan of the city is inherited from the Romans, while the handsome Georgian streets – it's one of the UK's best-preserved Georgian cities – fan out from **Chichester (market) Cross**, which dates from 1501. It's a friendly, vibrant city, where ancient history and Georgian elegance combine with a 21st-century cosmopolitan vibe.

Not surprisingly, the best place to start is magnificent 12th-century **Chichester Cathedral** (free), the seat of the Church of England Diocese of Chichester. Consecrated in 1108, the cathedral has stood at the centre of Chichester for over 900 years, its unique architecture reflecting just about every century of its life, where original medieval features sit alongside contemporary artworks. Look out for the Arundel Tomb (subject of a Philip Larkin poem) and two beautiful 12th-century carved stone panels, the Chichester Reliefs. There's also a stained-glass window by Marc Chagall and a striking John Piper tapestry behind the high altar. Also, take some time to explore the cloisters and surrounding church buildings, which are very attractive.

Marc Chagall window

From the cathedral it's just a few steps to the award-winning **Novium Museum** (free), which has three floors of exhibitions and artefacts and is a must-see for anyone with an interest in Chichester's fascinating history. Built on the site of the old Roman baths, which fill most of the

Chichester Cathedral

ground floor, the museum tells the story of Chichester through both permanent and temporary exhibitions. If Roman history is your bag, a mile outside the city is **Fishbourne Roman Palace** (fee), once the largest Roman villa north of the Alps.

Pallant House Gallery

A short distance away in North Pallant (lined with gorgeous buildings) is **Pallant House Gallery** (fee) and restaurant, located in a handsome Grade I listed Queen Anne house. The modern airy extension houses a superb collection of 20th-century British art by the likes of Frank Auerbach, Peter Blake, Patrick Caulfield, Lucian Freud, Ben Nicholson, Eduardo Paolozzi, John Piper and Graham Sutherland, alongside temporary exhibitions. A bit further north is the **Oxmarket Gallery** (free) in St Andrew's Court, a charity staging over 150 exhibitions a year in a Grade II listed medieval church.

Chichester's main green space is beautiful **Priory Park**, enclosed on two sides by the imposing Roman city walls and home to an aviary, lawn bowls and a nice café (see **Food & Drink**). The park also contains the Grade I listed **Guildhall**, dating from 1282, and the remains of a Norman motte. Next to Chichester Cathedral is the beautifully maintained **Bishop's Palace Gardens** (free), bordered by the city walls and the Tudor wall, from where you can enjoy superb views of the cathedral and the handsome 13th-century Bishop's Palace (private).

City Walls

One of the best ways to familiarise yourself with the city is to take a stroll around the 1,800-year-old city walls, some 80 per cent of which are still intact. The 1½-mile tree-lined trail around the top of the walls encircles the historic centre of the city, visiting award-winning parks and offering fine views.

Sleepy Chichester isn't noted for its sparkling entertainment or nightlife, but it does have the magnificent **Chichester Festival Theatre**, one of the country's best regional theatres with regular West End transfers. If it's music you're after, you can enjoy

Bishop's Palace Gardens

Food & Drink

- **Fenwicks Café:** Situated in Priory Park, licensed Fenwicks serves delicious locally sourced food in a lovely setting (daily 9.30am-5.30pm, £).

- **Field & Fork:** A family-run restaurant housed in a historic building near Priory Park serving delicious seasonal British cuisine; the set market menu is good value (01243-789915, Tue-Sat lunch noon-2.45pm, closed Sun, Mon, ££).

- **St Martin's Organic Coffee House:** Award-winning vegetarian-friendly café, located in a handsome 18th-century house with log fires and a glorious garden (01243-786715, Tue-Sat 10am-6pm, closed Sun-Mon, £).

performances throughout the year by world-renowned musicians, orchestras and choirs. The city stages a celebrated four-week arts and music festival (**Festival of Chichester**) in June-July, and is also home to a huge variety of restaurants and gastropubs.

If you're planning on staying for a few days, then the area around Chichester offers a wealth of attractions on its doorstep, including boat trips on the **Chichester Canal**, the world-famous Goodwood estate (2.4mi), charming **Bosham** village (5mi, see page 64), West Dean Gardens (6mi), the seaside resort of Bognor Regis (7mi) and magnificent Arundel Castle (11mi), to name just a few. Nature lovers will appreciate the superb South Downs National Park to the north of the city and **Chichester Harbour**, an area of outstanding natural beauty (AONB), noted for its marine birdlife.

Chichester Harbour

Colchester

Address: Colchester, Essex CO1 1PJ
(visitcolchester.com)
Rail: from 50min via Liverpool Street station
Road: 1h 35min (67mi) via A12
Nearby: East Bergholt, Dedham Vale, **Mersea
Island**

Roman Theatre, Colchester (artist's impression)

Situated on the River Colne in Essex, Colchester is a historic market town 67 miles northeast of London, the second largest town (after Norwich) in East Anglia. Dating from AD43, it's the oldest recorded Roman town in Britain (allegedly the oldest town in Britain full stop) and, for a period, was the capital of Roman Britain (*Camulodunum*). It was burnt to the ground by Boudicca's Iceni tribe a few decades later and never regained its former prominence. After the fall of the Roman Empire in AD410, Colchester passed through the hands of the Saxons, Vikings and Normans.

Where better to start than with the Romans, whose history can be seen throughout the town. Colchester's Roman wall is the oldest and longest surviving town wall in Britain, built AD65-80 to defend the town after the Boudican rebellion in AD60, and includes Balkerne Gate, the original main entrance to the town. A circular walk of two miles follows the course of the wall and its surviving parts. Off Maidenburgh Street are the remains of a **Roman Theatre**, while in 2005 the only known Roman circus in Britain was discovered just north of Abbey Field, which would have seated up to 8,000 spectators.

Colchester Castle

Castle Museum

Water Tower

The town's most prominent historic building and main attraction is **Colchester Castle** (fee), built on the remains of the Roman Temple of Claudius. Founded by William the Conqueror, the castle was built around the same time as the Tower of London. The **Castle Museum** (fee) features a superb exhibition of Roman history and artefacts, including the stunning Fenwick Hoard of Roman jewellery discovered in 2014. The town also boasts Saxon and Norman churches, and countless timber-framed houses and buildings, some of which still bear bullet-holes and scars from the English Civil War. Also worth a look are the ruins of **St Botolph's Priory**, which are close to the railway station. More recent buildings include Britain's oldest Victorian **Water Tower**

Castle Park

Dutch Quarter

Some of Colchester's most picturesque streets are in the so-called **Dutch Quarter**. In the 16th century Colchester was home to many Flemish Protestant refugees fleeing religious persecution, although the houses actually pre-date their arrival and were formerly inhabited by the Jewish community and other immigrants. Today, it's a quiet residential area just north of the High Street.

(1883), close to the Balkerne Gate, and the splendid Baroque **Town Hall**, opened in 1902, which features a 162ft tower and magnificent function rooms.

Colchester is home to a number of museums, in addition to the Castle Museum. Also in Colchester Castle Park is **Hollytrees Museum** (free), a social history museum occupying a handsome 18th-century Georgian townhouse. It contains a wide range of local curios, including a collection of longcase clocks and a fabulous dolls' house replica of the museum itself. Nearby on the High Street is the **Natural History Museum** (free), located in the former All Saints' Church. Also worth a visit is **Firstsite**, an innovative arts and cultural centre housed in a striking curved building, designed by the Uruguayan architect Rafael Viñoly.

Food & Drink

- **Greyfriars:** Superb hotel restaurant with an Art Deco feel, serving modern European cuisine. Good value table d'hôte lunch, including Sunday roast (01206-575913, lunch noon-2.30pm, Sun lunch noon-4pm, ££).

- **Loofer's:** Calling itself a 'food & coffee place', Loofer's is a popular café serving Mediterranean influenced food (Mon-Sat 8am-6pm, Sun 10am-5pm, £).

- **Purple Dog:** One of Colchester's oldest pubs dating from around 1647, PD offers award-winning ales and tasty homemade food (01206-564995, 9.30/11am-11pm/1.30am, £).

Nearby, the **Minories Galleries** is a contemporary art gallery in a listed Georgian building, run by the Colchester School of Art.

Colchester Castle Park is blessed with over 600 mature trees and has the River Colne flowing through its northern section, where there are some nice waterside walks. It also features a number of beautiful gardens. **Avignon Garden** commemorates the twinning of Colchester with Avignon in France in 1972, while the **Wetzlar Garden** (1979) celebrates its twinning with the German city of Wetzlar in 1969. Located to the side of Hollytrees Museum, the Wetzlar Garden is a traditional garden constructed around a central water feature, and leads into the Sensory Garden, a walkway between

raised flower beds designed so that the plants provide colour and scent, while the surrounding mosaics are appealing to touch. Around four miles outside the town is **Colchester Zoo**, home to many rare and endangered species, while the world-famous **Beth Chatto Gardens** are six miles away.

If it's entertainment you're after, the flourishing **Colchester Arts Centre**, a multi-function arts venue located in the former St Mary-at-the-Walls church (1872), is home to the repertory **Mercury Theatre**, offering a comprehensive programme of music, performance and comedy. Colchester also has two amateur theatres, the **Headgate Theatre** and the university **Lakeside Theatre**.

There's plenty to keep your tastebuds tickled, from traditional pubs to inviting cafés, fast food to fine dining, while shopaholics will be delighted with the town's wide range of independent shops and markets. If possible, try to time your trip to include the weekly market (Fri-Sat) and/or the farmers' market (first Fri of the month).

St Botolph's Priory

Faversham

Address: Faversham, Kent ME13 7AE (visitfaversham.org)

Rail: from 1h 8min via Cannon Street, St Pancras International and Victoria stations

Road: 1h 30min (53mi) via M2

Nearby: Canterbury, Isle of Sheppey, North Downs AONB, **Whitstable**

One of England's most charming and historic market towns, Faversham in Kent is 53 miles southeast of London, lying next to the Swale, a creek separating mainland Kent from the Isle of Sheppey in the Thames (Swale) Estuary. There has been a settlement at Faversham since pre-Roman times, next to the ancient sea port on Faversham Creek. The town is located close to the A2, which follows the ancient Roman Watling Street, although it's first mentioned in a royal charter of 811, when it was described as the King's Town.

Faversham's main claim to fame is its abundance of historic timber-framed buildings – around 500 are listed by English Heritage – most of which are located in a large conservation area. **Abbey Street**, which dates from the 13th century, has been described as the finest medieval street in southeast England, while Court Street, Tanners Street and West Street transport you back to the 16th century. North of the town at the end of Abbey Street is Standard Quay, a collection of quirky little shops in old barns overlooking the picturesque creek.

Arden's House, Abbey Street

Other buildings worth seeking out include a pair of 15th-century barns at **Abbey Farm** and **Arden's House** in Abbey Street, once part of Faversham's Benedictine Abbey founded by King Stephen in 1148. **Faversham Parish Church, St Mary of Charity** (Grade I listed) was established in 1147 and has a distinctive crown spire added in the late 18th century and an interior restored by Sir George Gilbert Scott in the mid-19th century. The **Guildhall** in Market Place was built as a market hall in

Standard Quay

1574 and has been used by market traders for almost 450 years, while the Faversham Almshouses were founded and endowed by Thomas Mendfield in 1614 (rebuilt in the 19th century with a bequest from Henry Wreight). For those who prefer slightly more recent architecture, there's an abundance of Georgian and Victorian buildings to admire, too.

Gunpowder factories were established in Faversham in the 16th century, and the town was the centre of the UK explosives industry from 1874 to 1919. An explosion in 1916 that killed over 100 people led to the decline of the industry, which closed in the '30s.

West Street

Faversham's main museum is at the **Fleur de Lis Heritage Centre** (fee) and tells the story of the town from the earliest archaeological times to today (the centre also hosts the town's Visitor Information Centre). A short distance southwest of the town centre is **Maison Dieu** (House of God, fee), a former hospital, monastery, hostel, retirement home and royal lodge commissioned by Henry III in 1234, now a museum managed by English Heritage.

The town's green spaces include the **Faversham Recreation Ground** to the east of the centre, established in 1860 by Henry Wreight, who bequeathed his estate to the town. To the north of the town is the **Oare Gunpowder Works Country Park**, where you

can see the remnants of the area's gunpowder industry, while further north on the estuary is the 176-acre **Oare Marshes Nature Reserve**, which is of international importance for migratory, over-wintering and breeding wetland birds. To the south of the town (close to the M2) is the **Brogdale Collections** (fee), home to the world's largest collection (4,000 varieties) of fruit trees and bushes.

The **Alexander Centre** in the town is a civic hub and community centre, housed in a beautiful Georgian building, while the **Royal Cinema** is one of only two surviving mock Tudor cinemas in the UK. The modern **Arden Theatre** is named after Thomas Arden (see **Arden's House** above) – a former mayor of Faversham who was murdered in 1551 by his wife and her lover – which inspired the first English domestic tragedy, *Arden of Faversham*. Also worth a visit is the town's **Shepherd Neame Brewery**, Britain's oldest brewery officially

Shepherd Neame Brewery

Food & Drink

- **Posillipo:** Acclaimed Italian (Neapolitan) restaurant overlooking Faversham Creek with a huge alfresco seating area (01795-590580, Mon-Sun noon-late, ££).
- **The Sun Inn:** 14th-century inn in the old town (with 12 boutique bedrooms) serving delicious fresh food (01795-535098, lunch noon-3pm, £).
- **The Yard:** Popular café in Jacob Yard offering fusion food and creative drinks, including gluten-free and vegetarian options (9am-4pm, Sun 9.30am-12.30pm, closed Mon, £).

Faversham Creek

founded in 1698, where you can take a tour and enjoy tastings!

Faversham is home to an abundance of independent shops, including the celebrated **Macknade Fine Foods** on the southeast edge of town, one of the country's leading food halls. Faversham Market (Tue, Fri-Sat) is the oldest street market in Kent, dating back over 900 years and still held in the town centre. There are also monthly markets in Preston Street and Court Street. When you fancy a snack or lunch, you'll find Faversham is home to a smorgasbord of eateries, with something to suit every pocket and taste.

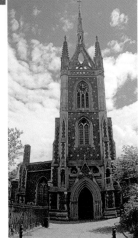

St Mary of Charity

Oxford

Address: Oxford OX1 1BX (oxfordcity.co.uk)

Rail: from 57min via Paddington or Marylebone stations

Road: 1h 30min (56mi) via M40 and A40

Nearby: Blenheim Palace, Chilterns, Cotswolds

College Visitor Information & Fees

For college opening times and fees (if applicable), see https://www.ox.ac.uk/visitors/visiting-oxford/visiting-the-colleges?wssl=1.

B est known for its world-famous university and forest of 'dreaming' spires, Oxford is the county town of Oxfordshire. Located 56 miles west of London on the River Thames (known locally as the River Isis) and its tributary the River Cherwell, it's a grand cosmopolitan city, steeped in history, privilege and prestige. First settled in Saxon times, it began as a river crossing around the year 900. Today, history and superb architecture – every period of English architecture is represented, from the late Saxon period to the 20th century – greet you around every corner. Oxford has more of a city feel than its academic rival Cambridge (see page 17), but its honey-coloured colleges and buildings are just as beautiful, and its superb museums are second only to London's.

Established in the 12th century, **Oxford University** (ox.ac.uk) is the oldest university in the English-speaking world, and one of the most prestigious, comprising 38 independent colleges scattered throughout the city. Most colleges open their doors to visitors – usually the college quad, gardens and chapel – and many are free to visit (see box). Some colleges also open their dining hall to visitors, such as Wadham College and Christ Church, whose grand hall was the setting for Hogwarts' Great Hall in the *Harry Potter* films. Christ Church (fee) is also home to a spectacular cathedral and incorporates Tom Tower, designed by Sir Christopher Wren. Needless to say, a tour of some of the hallowed university colleges is a must, the most popular of which include Christ Church, Trinity, Exeter, All Souls, Magdalen and New College.

Other iconic buildings include the **Bodleian Library** (see below), the **Radcliffe Camera** – camera meaning 'room' in Latin and now a reading room for the Bodleian Library – and the 15th-century **Divinity School**. Then there's the **Bridge of Sighs**, aka Hertford Bridge

Oxford Panorama

Bridge of Sighs

(modelled on the one in Venice), which joins two parts of Hertford College over New College Lane; the **Sheldonian Theatre** (Wren's first major design); the University Church of **St Mary the Virgin**, with its 13th-century Gothic tower; **Carfax Tower**, which is all that remains of 12th-century St Martin's Church; **Oxford Castle & Prison** (fee), built in Norman times; and beautiful **Oxford Town Hall**, a Jacobethan treasure from1897.

Oxford boasts more than its fair share of world-class museums, most of which are university departments. The first stop has to be the celebrated **Ashmolean Museum** (free). Britain's oldest public museum, established in

1683, it's home to an astoundingly diverse collection of artwork and objects from around the world. You can see everything from exquisite drawings by Renaissance master Raphael to modern Chinese paintings. Also worth a visit is quirky **Pitt Rivers Museum** (free), home to the university's archaeological and anthropological collections, housing over 600,000 objects, photographs and manuscripts from all periods of human existence, and the magnificent **Bodleian Library** (fee), the first library in Oxford, founded in the 1300s and containing over 12 million items.

Christ Church Picture Gallery (fee) is home to a wonderful collection of Old Master paintings and drawings,

Bodleian Library

including treasures by Filippino Lippi, Veronese, Anthony van Dyck, Leonardo, Dürer and Rubens. Other important collections include the Gothic Revival Museum of Natural History, the History of Science Museum, the Museum of Oxford, and the Bate Collection of musical instruments in the university's Faculty of Music, all of which offer free entrance. Oxford also boasts a thriving contemporary art scene, with many commercial art galleries.

Oxford is blessed with an abundance of green spaces, including **University Parks** (70 acres) in the heart of the city with a stunning collection

Radcliffe Camera

Food & Drink

- **The Bear Inn:** One of the oldest pubs in Oxford with a history going back to 1242 (the current building dates from the early 17th century), the Bear serves Fuller's ales and traditional pub grub (01865-728164, 11am-11pm/midnight, £).
- **Turl Street Kitchen:** Georgian restaurant with rustic tables and stripped floors, offering tasty modern British seasonal cuisine (01865-264171, 8am-11pm, 5pm Sun-Tue, £).
- **Vaults & Garden Café:** Superb café in the atmospheric former University Church of St Mary the Virgin, offering a changing organic menu, including vegetarian and vegan options. It has a lovely garden, too (01865-279112, 8.30am-6pm, £).

Ashmolean Museum

of trees and plants and a huge variety of walks. The city is rightly famous for its beautiful **Meadows**, which include the vast Port Meadow to the northwest bordering the River Thames, the Water Meadow, the Angel & Greyhound Meadow, Christ Church Meadow and more. The university's **Botanic Garden** (fee) – instituted in 1621, it's the UK's oldest – is a haven of tranquillity with exquisite plants from around the world. Then there's the splendid college gardens, most of which are open to the public, and a host of walks along the city's waterways. Over Magdalen Bridge and east of the city centre, 50-acre **South Park** hosts open-air concerts and circuses in summer.

Oriel College

All Souls College

For cutting-edge art visit Modern Art Oxford, one of the UK's most exciting contemporary art spaces featuring a changing programme of exhibitions and installations (mostly free).

Oxford has an enviable roll call of world-class venues for dance, drama and music, with around a dozen theatres and cinemas dotted across the city. The city has a vibrant music scene, a vast choice of lively bars and clubs, a wealth of irresistible historic pubs, and a huge range of restaurants and eateries – you really are spoilt for choice. If shopping is your bag, then Oxford is a nirvana, with a multitude of independent shops and boutiques and a fantastic covered market dating back to 1774.

It's a huge understatement to say Oxford offers far more than you can possibly hope to see in a day – all the more reason to start planning your next visit!

Port Meadow

Botanic Garden

River Cherwell

Rochester

> **Address:** Rochester, Kent ME1 1YD (visitmedway.org/see-and-do/destinations/rochester)
>
> **Rail:** from 37min via Blackfriars, St Pancras International and Victoria stations
>
> **Road:** 1h 10min (33mi) via A13 and A2
>
> **Nearby:** Chatham

Historic Rochester, with its Norman castle and ancient cathedral, is tucked into a bend on the River Medway in Kent, 33 miles southeast of London. Along with its neighbours – Chatham, Gillingham, Strood and a number of villages – it forms an area known as the Medway Towns. For centuries Rochester has been of vital strategic importance due to its position near the confluence of the Thames and the Medway. Neolithic remains have been found in the vicinity of the city, which has been occupied by Celts, Romans (who arrived in AD43), Jutes and Saxons.

Rochester Castle

At the heart of the town is majestic **Rochester Cathedral**, the second-oldest cathedral in England (after Canterbury), founded in 604 by Bishop Justus. The current Norman building dates from 1080, when it was built by the French monk, Gundulf, and has one of the finest Romanesque façades in England. It also features fine examples of later Gothic architecture, along with the splendid 14th-century chapter library door. Just south of the cathedral is the **King's School** – the king referred to is Henry VIII, although there has been a school here since 604, making it the second-oldest continuously operating school in the world.

Just across the road from the cathedral is one of the best-preserved and finest examples of Norman architecture in England, **Rochester Castle** (fee), whose great keep towers over the

Rochester Cathedral

HMS Gannet, Chatham

River Medway, where the Romans built the first bridge. Like the cathedral, the castle was begun by Bishop Gundulf in 1087, and it incorporates the remains of the Roman city walls which guarded the river crossing. The castle has a chequered history, having been subject to siege three times and partly demolished by King John in 1215. Just one mile from Rochester, the **Historic Dockyard** (fee) in Chatham – the most complete surviving dockyard from the age of sail in the world – is well worth a visit. Established in the mid-1500s, Chatham witnessed the beginning of the Royal Navy's long period of supremacy, and many famous warships were built here, including Nelson's flagship *HMS Victory*.

Other buildings of note include **Restoration House** (fee), a famous city mansion where Charles II stayed on the eve of the restoration of the monarchy in 1660 – it featured as Miss Havisham's Satis House in Charles Dickens' novel *Great Expectations*. Also immortalised by Dickens was the **Six Poor Travellers' House** (free), a Tudor charity 'hotel'; Grade I listed **Eastgate House** (fee), a 16-17th-century town house with a rich history; **Dickens' Swiss Chalet**, where the author wrote some of his greatest works, located in the gardens of Eastgate House; and **Rochester Guildhall** built in 1687, which has a magnificent plaster ceiling and an amazing weather vane featuring a fully-rigged, 18th-century warship. Across the river from Rochester (in Strood) is 13th-century **Temple Manor** (free), a rare surviving 13th-century house that once belonged to the Knights Templar.

The Guildhall is home to the excellent **Guildhall Museum** (free) of local history, founded in 1897, which tells the fascinating history of the Medway, including the life and times of Charles Dickens. Rochester is also home to the **Huguenot Museum** (fee), Britain's only museum of Huguenot history, while in nearby Chatham is the **Royal Engineers Museum** (fee), Kent's largest military museum.

Rochester has some delightful green spaces, including the **Castle Gardens** and the **Garth**, a tranquil place for reflection near the cathedral where

Rochester Panorama

Food & Drink

- **The Coopers Arms:** A characterful pub since 1543 occupying a 12th-century building, offering good food, fine ales and a pretty garden (01634-404298, Sun-Thu noon-11pm, Fri-Sat noon-midnight, £).
- **Elizabeth's Restaurant:** Long established, family-run restaurant in a 16th-century Tudor building, serving delicious European cuisine (01634-843471, lunch Tue-Sun noon-2pm, closed Mon, ££).
- **Tiny Tim's Tea Rooms:** Popular café just off the High Street serving everything from breakfast and lunch to afternoon tea – plus delicious cakes and scones (Mon-Fri 9am-6pm, £).

beautiful small park with majestic trees. In the south of the city are the expansive green spaces of **Jackson's Field** and **Victoria Gardens**. Nature lovers may wish to visit the nearby spectacular **North Kent Marshes**, one of the most important natural wetlands in northern Europe for migrating birds.

Charles Dickens

Rochester is closely associated with novelist Charles Dickens (1812-1870), who spent his childhood in Medway and returned to the area later as a successful writer. He featured the town in many of his works and many buildings he depicted can still be seen today.

Bishop Gundulf built his priory. **The Esplanade** and **Churchfields** bordering the Medway comprise a large expanse of grassland with some attractive walks, while **The Vines** next to Restoration House (see above) is a

Rochester isn't particularly noted for its cultural activities (the Georgian Royal Theatre is now an events centre), although the amateur **Medway Little Theatre** on the High Street keeps theatrical traditions alive. The city stages a number of concerts and festivals throughout the year, including the celebrated **Sweeps Festival** in May, which recreates the chimney sweeps' traditional holiday, and two **Dickens Festivals**. Rochester (and the Medway district) offers a wide choice of restaurants to suit every pocket, plus an abundance of notable pubs, while the quaint Victorian High Street contains many original independent shops and there's a monthly farmers' market nearby.

Guildhall Museum

Rye

Address: Rye, East Sussex TN31 7HE (cometorye.co.uk, ryesussex.co.uk)

Rail: from 1h 8min to Ashford International (change for Rye) via St Pancras International station

Road: 2h (77mi) via A2 and M20

Nearby: Dungeness, Great Dixter House & Gardens, **Hastings**, Dungeness, High Weald AONB, Winchelsea

An ancient market town 77 miles southeast of London, picturesque Rye in East Sussex is situated at the confluence of three rivers: the Rother, the Tillingham and the Brede. Rye was part of the Saxon Manor of Rameslie, which was given to the Benedictine Abbey of Fécamp in Normandy by King Ethelred and remained in Norman hands until 1247. In the 18th century the town was one of the refuges of the notorious Hawkhurst Gang of smugglers, whose boltholes included the town's Mermaid and Ye Olde Bell inns. Rye was once a seaport – it was a member of the famous Cinque Ports (see box, page 42) – but the silting up of the River Rother stranded the town two miles inland.

Today, Rye is one of the best-preserved medieval towns in England, with a profusion of higgledy-piggledy, half-timbered houses and jumble of steep cobbled lanes. Notable buildings include the famous **Mermaid Inn** (see **Food & Drink**) with a history going back to 1156 – the current building dates from 1420 but the cellars are the 12th-century originals – while charming **Ye Olde Bell Inn** was built in 1390. Other highlights include **Oak Corner**, near the bottom of Mermaid Street, a private dwelling from 1377, rebuilt in 1490. The **Landgate**, dating from 1329, is the only surviving gate of four original fortified entrances to the town, and remains the only vehicular access to the medieval centre. A relative newcomer, the **Old Rye Grammar School** was founded in 1636 as a free school, and was in use until 1908.

Mermaid Street

One of the oldest buildings in Rye is **Ypres Tower** (fee), aka Rye Castle. It was built in 1249 under

Mermaid Inn

Landgate

Henry III as 'Baddings Tower' to defend the town from the French and later named after its owner, John de Ypres (pronounced 'Wipers' by locals!). Over the centuries it has been used for defence, as a private home, a prison and a mortuary, and is now home to **Rye Museum** (fee) where you can learn about the town's rich history. Also well worth a visit is magnificent 12th-century **St Mary's Church**, sometimes referred to as the 'cathedral of East Sussex'. The church has some lovely stained-glass windows and one of the oldest functioning church turret clocks in the country, installed around 1561-2 in the Quarter Boys clock tower (so called because it strikes the quarters but not the hours). You can climb the tower (fee) to see the clock mechanism and church bells, and enjoy panoramic views of the surrounding countryside.

Cinque Ports

The origins of the Cinque Ports can be traced back to Anglo-Saxon times, although it wasn't until 1100 that the term came into general use. In 1155, a royal charter established the ports to maintain ships ready for the crown in times of need. By the reign of Henry II (1154-1189), the towns of Hastings, New Romney, Hythe, Dover and Sandwich were known collectively as the Cinque Ports, while Rye and Winchelsea were known as 'Ancient Towns' and were added later.

Rye has many literary and artistic connections, one of which is **Lamb House** (National Trust, fee), built in 1722 by James Lamb. An early visitor was George I when a storm drove his ship ashore at Camber in 1726. From 1897, Lamb House was the home of American author Henry James, who wrote three novels while living in Rye, and between 1918 and 1940 it was the base for English novelist E. F. Benson who set his *Mapp & Lucia* novels in and around Rye. The handsome red-brick fronted house has a beautiful walled garden and is wonderfully tranquil. The **Rye Heritage Centre**, located in a 19th-century sail loft on the quayside, is home to the 'Story of Rye', a unique *son et lumière*, employing a scale model of Victorian Rye to bring to life over 700 years of history.

When you've had your fill of the town's gorgeous architecture and require sustenance, Rye offers an abundance of fine restaurants, cosy inns, modern coffee shops and traditional tea rooms. If shopping is your bag, the town has a host of interesting independent shops, a weekly farmers' market, and a thriving antiques and art scene.

Ypres Tower (Rye Castle)

Food & Drink

• **Cobbles Tea Room:** Popular tea room with courtyard serving delicious cakes, light lunches and afternoon tea (9am-5pm, £).

• **Mermaid Inn:** A characterful 15th-century smugglers' inn with 31 rooms, the Mermaid is an excellent choice for lunch (01797-223065; lunch noon-2.30pm, ££).

• **Ypres Castle Inn:** Beautiful 17th-century inn by the castle with a cosy interior and beer garden, serving tasty food and ales (01797-223248, noon-11pm, £).

Rye rooftops

A couple of miles out of town, magnificent **Rye Harbour Nature Reserve** is worth a visit, extending to 1,150 acres of wetlands, salt marshes and coastline, encompassing the ruins of 16th-century **Camber Castle** (fee) built by Henry VIII. One of Britain's most important conservation areas, the reserve is home to 4,500 different species, including some 300 bird varieties.

Rye Harbour

Lamb House

Saffron Walden

Address: Saffron Walden, Essex CB10 1HL
(visitsaffronwalden.gov.uk)

Rail: from 53min to Audley End via Liverpool
Street, then bus/taxi (10-20m)

Road: 1h 25min (57mi) via M11

Nearby: Audley End House, Bishop's Stortford,
Duxford (Imperial War Museum)

Saffron Walden is a delightful medieval market town in northwest Essex, 57 miles north of London, in an area settled from prehistoric times. The street layout you see today follows the course of the bailey enclosure of 12th-century **Walden Castle** (only the ruins remain) built by Geoffrey de Mandeville, Earl of Essex, who also established the first market in 1141.

Castle Street

St Mary's Church

This archetypal English town is one of the finest preserved examples of a medieval market town in the UK, with a rich heritage of ancient buildings. Fine examples of medieval timber-framed buildings can be seen in **Bridge Street** and **Castle Street**, where many buildings feature elaborate patterns of pargetting, a type of exterior plasterwork common to the area. One of the oldest and most intriguing timber-framed buildings is the former youth hostel at **1 Myddylton Place**, which dates back to at least the 15th century. Nearby **St Mary's Church** is the largest, and one of the most beautiful, parish churches in Essex; its current incarnation, begun around 1450, is one of the best examples of Perpendicular architecture in East Anglia.

Saffron

The original name of the town was simply 'Walden' – the Saffron prefix was added when it became a centre for cultivating crocuses in the 16th-17th centuries. The valuable extract from the stigmas was used in medicines, as a condiment, in perfume, as an aphrodisiac and as a yellow dye, but the industry died out at the end of the 18th century.

15th-century cottage

No visit to Saffron Walden would be complete without seeing Jacobean **Audley End House** (fee), built by Thomas, Lord Audley (c 1488-1544), Lord Chancellor under Henry VIII. Now owned by English Heritage, the mansion (1.6 miles from the town centre) was created from the monastic buildings of Walden Priory, which Audley purchased from the king. Audley's house was completely rebuilt in the early 17th century to create the magnificent Jacobean mansion you see today. The interior is exquisitely decorated with a superb collection of fine furniture and art, while the beautiful gardens are dotted with follies and bridges designed by Robert Adam.

Saffron Walden Museum (fee) occupies one of the oldest purpose-built museum buildings in the country, dating from 1835, containing everything from mammoth tusks to mummies, an early Tudor bed to Samurai armour. The award-winning museum explores the archaeology, natural history and social history of northwest Essex and the wider world. In the attractive grounds of the museum are the ruins of the 12th-century castle keep.

The **Fry Art Gallery** (free) on Castle Street houses a unique collection of works by the Great Bardfield group of artists, who settled in the Essex countryside in the '30s. The public **Exchange Gallery** on the first floor of the library stages a rolling programme of

Amazing

Saffron Walden is unique in the UK in having two historic mazes: the Victorian hedge maze in Bridge End Gardens (shown) and the turf labyrinth on the Common (there are also two modern mazes). They are celebrated in a Maze Festival.

exhibitions, while the **Saffron Walden Gallery** at the top of the High Street is a contemporary art gallery offering original art, ceramics, sculpture and glassware.

On the north side of town are beautiful **Bridge End Gardens** (Grade II* listed, free), laid out around 1840 by Francis Gibson. He designed the gardens as a series of rooms, each with its own unique character. Recently restored to their former glory, they contain a formal rose garden, walled garden, kitchen garden, sunken Dutch

Market Square

garden, wilderness and a wonderful yew hedge maze. The maze theme continues just off Hill Street in **Jubilee Garden**, where the floor of the bandstand features a labyrinth design with a sleeping hare in the central octagon, while **Dorset House Garden** (off Church Street) contains *The Children of Calais* (2018), a bronze by local artist Ian Wolter portraying six children as refugees, their poses echoing Auguste Rodin's famous sculpture *The Burghers of Calais*. The **Common** is an expansive open space in the town centre with a historic turf labyrinth on its easternmost side which has history going back to 1699.

In recent years Saffron Walden has become a major centre for the arts, with the opening of the **Saffron Hall** in 2013 and the earlier **Saffron Screen**, a popular, not-for-profit, independent cinema. Saffron Hall is an award-winning, 740-seat performance space that hosts an annual season of concerts and events featuring national and international artists. If you fancy a bit of retail therapy, the street market is held on Tuesdays and Saturdays, while the town also has many interesting independent shops. When you fancy a bite to eat, Saffron Walden offers a wide range of options to suit all tastes and budgets.

Food & Drink

• **Cross Keys Hotel:** Boutique hotel on the High Street housed in a splendid 12th-century building with a terrace, serving delicious food from breakfast to dinner (01799-522207, 7am-11pm, £).

• **The Eight Bells:** Cosy 16th-century pub with a nice garden offering superb (local) seasonal food, including all-day Sunday roast (01799-522790, lunch noon-3pm, Sun noon-6pm, £).

• **Te Amo:** Popular café and vintage tea room on Cross Street serving breakfast, lunch and afternoon tea (9.30am-4.30pm, closed Sun, £).

Audley End House

Salisbury

Address: Salisbury, Wiltshire SP1 1EJ
(visitwiltshire.co.uk/salisbury)

Rail: from 1h 22min via Waterloo station

Road: 1h 55min (88mi) via M3

Nearby: Beaulieu, New Forest, Old Sarum,
Stonehenge, Winchester

Most famous for its beautiful 13th-century cathedral, Salisbury is located in Wiltshire on the edge of Salisbury Plain, 88 miles southwest of London. The original site of the city (called **Old Sarum**) was two miles north and consisted of an Iron Age hill fort that was reused by the Romans, Saxons and Normans; remnants of the old fort remain, along with castle ruins and the foundations of the original cathedral, and can be explored (fee). Tensions between the church and army led to the cathedral being relocated two miles south to New Sarum, around which Salisbury grew up.

Salisbury Cathedral (1220-1258) is renowned for its magnificent soaring spire and is one of the UK's leading examples of Early English architecture. The spire dates from 1549 and at 404ft is the tallest in the UK. The cathedral has the UK's largest cloisters and is set within the largest cathedral close (80 acres) in Britain, while the cathedral clock (allegedly dating from 1386) is among the oldest working examples in the world. It's free to visit the cathedral although there's a charge to climb the tower.

The main entrance to Cathedral Close is guarded by the splendid 14th-century **High Street Gate** – still locked at night (11pm-6am) – which housed a small jail for those convicted of misdeeds within the Liberty of the Close. Just inside the gate stands the **College**

Salisbury Cathedral

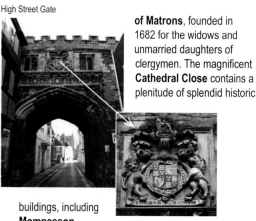

High Street Gate

of Matrons, founded in 1682 for the widows and unmarried daughters of clergymen. The magnificent **Cathedral Close** contains a plenitude of splendid historic buildings, including **Mompesson House** (fee), an 18th-century National Trust mansion; attractive **Arundells** (fee), dating back to the 13th century (though extensively rebuilt in the 18th), and the former home of Prime Minister Sir Edward Heath; and the 13th-century **Medieval Hall**, the setting for splendid banquets, just 200m from the cathedral. South of the cathedral is the **Bishop's Palace**, now the private Cathedral School, parts of which date back to 1220. The Close is also home to several museums (see below).

Other important buildings and sites in Salisbury include charming **St Thomas's Church**, the original of which was built for cathedral workmen in 1219 and named after Thomas Becket. The current church dates from the 15th century and features the celebrated Doom Painting above the chancel arch, painted around 1475 and depicting Christ on the Day of Judgement. The **Poultry Cross** at the junction of Silver and Minster Streets is a 14th-century (Grade I listed) market cross. If you have time, the World Heritage Site of **Stonehenge** (eight miles north, see page 184) is a must-see.

Salisbury has a number of museums and galleries. The **Salisbury Museum** (fee) is an excellent local history museum housed in 13th-century King's House within the Cathedral Close, while nearby the **Rifles Berkshire & Wiltshire Museum** (fee) is situated in The Wardrobe, a 15th-century building used to store the robes of the Bishop of Salisbury. The city also has a number of galleries, including the **Young Gallery** (free) in the central library, Gallery 21, Whitewall Galleries and **Fisherton Mill**. The latter is in a former Victorian grain mill and contains galleries, artists' studios and a popular café.

Magna Carta

Displayed in the cathedral's **Chapter House** is the best-preserved of the four surviving original copies of the *Magna Carta*, a charter of rights agreed to by King John at Runnymede on 15th June 1215.

If you wish to stretch your legs, Salisbury offers a number of parks and gardens. Among the most popular is **Queen Elizabeth Gardens**, a glorious formal garden

Arundells

with famous views of the cathedral to the east and the River Avon to the south; from here you can access the Town Path which leads to **Harnham Water Meadows** and on to Harnham village – a serene and lovely walk. Around a mile to the southeast is **Churchill Gardens**, also bordered by the Avon, home to a wide variety of shrubs and trees. Close to the town centre are the **Greencroft** and **Bourne Hill Gardens**, while to the north is attractive **Victoria Park**, the oldest park in Salisbury (1887), with formal planting and good sports facilities.

Salisbury's largest live entertainment venue is **City Hall**, which stages music, comedy and other performances, while **Salisbury Playhouse** is one of Britain's leading provincial theatres, or for a more intimate experience there's the bijou **Studio Theatre** with just 92 seats. Wiltshire Creative organises the celebrated annual **Salisbury International Arts Festival** at the end of May and beginning of June. When you're peckish Salisbury offers a bounty of places to eat and drink, while if you fancy a bit of retail therapy the city has an abundance of independent shops along with the historic **Charter Market** (Tue, Sat, 9am-3/4pm) in Market Place.

Food & Drink

- **Greengages Café:** Styling itself a coffee house and restaurant, Greengages offers gluten-free, vegetarian and vegan options (8am-5pm, closed Sun, £).

- **Haunch of Venison:** Historic (haunted) pub in a 14th-century building serving superb gastro food (01722-411313, 11am-10pm/midnight, £-££).

- **The New Inn:** Traditional (12th-century!) English pub in New Street offering tasty food and award-winning Badger ales (01722-326662, lunch noon-2.30pm, Sun 3pm, £).

Salisbury Cathedral from the Water Meadows

Salisbury Museum (King's House)

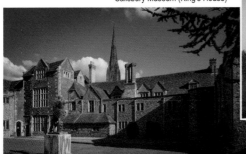

St Albans

> **Address:** St Albans, Herts AL1 3JE
> (enjoystalbans.com)
>
> **Rail:** from 18min via St Pancras International station
>
> **Road:** 1h (25mi) via M1
>
> **Nearby:** Hatfield House, Knebworth House, Woburn Safari Park

St Albans in Hertfordshire is a historic market town 25 miles northwest of London on the River Ver. It was the first major town (*Verulamium*) on the old Roman Watling Street and the second largest in Britain after *Londinium*. St Albans takes its name from the first recorded British saint, Alban, who lived in the town during the 3rd or 4th century and was beheaded by the Romans for his Christian beliefs. He was commemorated by an abbey, founded in the 8th century – built on the site where Saint Alban was buried – making it the oldest site of continuous Christian worship in Britain.

Today, St Albans is a classic English town, with Roman remains, ancient buildings, a thriving market, handsome parks and gardens, historic pubs and superb restaurants. Its skyline is dominated by the **Cathedral and Abbey Church of St Alban** – it officially ceased to be an abbey in the 16th century and became a cathedral in 1877. Built 1077-89, its architecture is a blend of Norman, Gothic and Victorian era restoration, with the longest nave in England.

St Alban

The great tower contains bricks salvaged from the ruins of Roman *Verulamium* and is the only 11th-century great crossing tower remaining in England. The cathedral's shrine to St Alban attracts pilgrims from far and wide, and on the Saturday closest to 22nd June – St Albans Day – there's a spectacular Pilgrimage Procession of giant puppets that tells the story of the saint's martyrdom.

St Albans Cathedral

Great Gateway of the Monastery

example of its kind in Britain, being a theatre with a stage rather than an amphitheatre. Subsequent excavations have revealed a row of Roman shop foundations, a villa and a secret shrine, all thought to date from the 1st century AD. Nearby, Verulamium Park contains remains of the city's ancient **Roman Wall** and the **Hypocaust**, part of a large AD200 Roman townhouse showing the early sophisticated heating system that allowed hot air to circulate beneath the mosaic floors and through the walls of a building. Later iconic buildings include the Neo-Classical Court House (1830), aka the **Old Town Hall**, now home to St Albans Museum.

Other historic buildings in and around St Albans include charming **St Michael's Church**, close to Verulamium Park, built in the 10th or early 11th century and the most significant surviving Saxon building in Britain. On the High Street, the **Clock Tower** was completed in 1405 and is the only medieval town belfry in England. Near the cathedral is the imposing **Great Gateway of the Monastery**, built in 1365 and the last remaining building (except for the Abbey itself) of the Benedictine Monastery, now the entrance to St Albans School, a public school dating back to the 10th century.

Not surprisingly, the city contains a profusion of Roman ruins, including a **Roman Theatre** built around AD140 and unearthed in 1847; it's the only visible

---

Hot Cross Buns

The Hot Cross Bun is said to originate in St Albans, where Brother Thomas Rodcliffe, a 14th-century monk at St Albans Abbey, developed an original recipe and began distributing buns to the poor on Good Friday in 1361.

There are two main museums in St Albans, the **St Albans Museum + Gallery** (free), opened in 2018 in the magnificent Old Town Hall, and the Verulamium Museum. Set over three floors, the St Albans Museum showcases over 2,000 years of heritage and contemporary artworks, including the building's historic rooms. At the **Verulamium Museum** (fee) you can explore Roman life, view recreated Roman rooms and admire some of the finest mosaics outside the Mediterranean. You can also see recent discoveries such as the Sandridge Hoard, a collection of 159 Roman gold coins found in a nearby field in 2012.

St Michael's Church

Food & Drink

- **George Street Canteen:** A cosy café with cathedral views, alfresco dining and tasty food (8.30am-4/5pm, £).
- **Lussmanns:** Overlooking Vintry Garden, Lussmanns is part of a small chain serving delicious modern British cuisine (01727-851941, noon-9pm/10.30pm, £-££).
- **Ye Olde Fighting Cocks:** Laying claim to be Britain's oldest pub – it's said to have 8th-century foundations – this historic pub serves delicious pub grub and a great Sunday lunch (01727-869152, noon-10.30pm/midnight, £-££).

can still be seen. An outstanding feature of the park is ornamental Verulam Lake, alongside the River Ver, constructed in 1929 and home to an abundance of water birds and one of the few heronries in Hertfordshire. Close to the cathedral is historic **Vintry Garden**, a walled garden and vineyard originally tended by medieval monks.

The main entertainment centre in St Albans is the **Alban Arena** (formerly St Albans City Hall), a theatre and music venue. Other venues include the **Maltings Arts Theatre**, a lively fringe theatre; the **Abbey Theatre**, a 230-seat theatre and studio space; and **St Albans Organ Theatre**, which contains a unique collection of mechanical (self-playing) musical instruments.

St Albans has been an important market town for centuries, with the street market (Wed, Sat) in St Peter's Street dating back to the 9th century, complemented by a wealth of independent shops. And when you're hungry or fancy a drink, the city offers a cornucopia of excellent restaurants, cafés and pubs – plus street food on market days.

The largest green space in St Albans is magnificent **Verulamium Park** (100 acres), where remains of the Roman city walls and the outline of the London Gate

Verulamium Park

Verulamium Museum

Winchester

> **Address:** Winchester, Hants SO23 9LJ
> (visitwinchester.co.uk)
>
> **Rail:** from 57min via Waterloo station
>
> **Road:** 1h 30min (68mi) via M3
>
> **Nearby: Beaulieu**, Chawton House, **New Forest**,
> Southampton, South Downs

Located on the edge of the South Downs National Park, 68 miles southwest of London, and straddling the River Itchen, Winchester is one of the UK's most historic cities. It developed from the Roman town of *Venta Belgarum*, which was formerly a Celtic fortified town. Winchester reached its zenith in the 9th century under King Alfred the Great (c 847-899) – King of the Anglo-Saxons (his statue is at the eastern end of The Broadway) – who made it his capital, and its prominence continued under the Normans, who built its magnificent cathedral.

Winchester Cathedral (fee, free on Sundays) is one of the largest in Europe, with the greatest overall length of any Gothic cathedral. It's also an outstanding example of all the main phases of English church architecture from the 11th century until the early 16th century, when much of today's

Altar Screen

building was complete. Work began on the cathedral in 1079 and it was consecrated in 1093, although there have been many changes, additions and restorations over the ensuing centuries. Among the cathedral's many treasures are the Norman crypt, medieval carvings, 12th-century wall paintings, the splendid 15th-century stone altar screen (above), and the 17th-century

Winchester Cathedral

King Canute and William II were buried in Winchester Cathedral, Henry III was baptised there, and it's where Mary Tudor married Philip of Spain. It's also the last resting place of novelist Jane Austen (1775-1817) – she lived nearby at Chawton from 1809 and died in Winchester – who has a memorial in the north aisle of the nave.

Morley Library, which houses the beautiful illuminated Winchester Bible (1160-1175).

The Cathedral Close contains a number of historic buildings from the time when the cathedral was also a priory, including the 13th-century **Deanery**, 15th-century timber-framed **Cheyney Court**, and the **Pilgrim's Hall**, which is the earliest hammer-beamed building still standing in England, built to accommodate pilgrims to Saint Swithun's shrine. Near the western end of the High Street is the imposing **Great Hall** (fee), the only remaining part of Winchester Castle. The castle was

Great Hall & Round Table

built in 1067, and for over 100 years was the seat of government of the Norman kings. The hall is one of the finest surviving aisled halls of the 13th century (built 1222-1235) and contains the iconic symbol of medieval mythology, **King Arthur's Round Table**, originally constructed in the 13th century and repainted in its present form for Henry VIII.

Other notable buildings and structures in Winchester include the 15th-century **Butter Cross** on the High Street; **Hyde Abbey Gatehouse**, the sole remains of 12th-century Benedictine Hyde Abbey, and nearby Norman **St Bartholomew's Church**; the ruins of **Wolvesey Castle**, the bishop's palace during medieval times; 13th-century **St Swithun-upon-Kingsgate Church**, located above one of the (restored) city gates; **Winchester City Mill**, a working 18th-century corn mill with a 1,000-year history; the imposing Victorian **Guildhall** completed in 1873; and the serene **Hospital of St Cross** (one mile south of

Cheyney Court & King's Gate

Hospital of St Cross

Museum, the Rifles Museum, the Gurkha Museum, and the Guardroom Museum (the Museum of the Adjutant-General's Corps). The **Westgate Museum** (free) is housed in the last remaining 12th-century gate into the city, which doubled as a debtors' prison for 150 years.

Winchester offers an abundance of entertainment options, including three theatres: the Theatre Royal, the Chesil Theatre and the Discovery Centre theatre. The **Theatre Royal** is the city's flagship venue, presenting drama, dance, children's theatre, comedy, music and pantomime in a beautiful Edwardian-style auditorium. The intimate **Chesil Theatre** occupies St Peter's

the city) dating from 1132, one of England's oldest continuing almshouses, still home to 25 'brothers'.

Winchester has a number of museums, including **Winchester City Museum** (free), which tells the story of England's ancient capital, from its origins as an Iron Age trading centre to Anglo-Saxon glory, the last journey of Jane Austen to the hunt for King Alfred's remains. The **Military Quarter**, the site of the 18th-century Peninsula Barracks, is home to Winchester's six **Military Museums** (fee for most) which are located within yards of each other. They are HorsePower (the Regimental Museum of The King's Royal Hussars), the Royal Hampshire Regiment Museum, the Royal Green Jackets

Food & Drink

• **Chesil Rectory:** Located in a magnificent building some 600 years old, with a nice courtyard garden, the Chesil offers classic modern British food (01962-851555, lunch noon-2.30pm, 3pm Sun, ££).

• **The Dispensary Kitchen:** A charming coffee shop/café in The Square near the cathedral, the Dispensary serves excellent breakfasts, coffee, pastries and light lunches (8am-4pm, Fri-Sat 8am-11pm, Sun 9am-4pm, £).

• **The Wykeham Arms:** A Fuller's pub in Kingsgate Street, the Wykeham is a gorgeous 18th-century country pub with rooms, offering tasty ales and quality seasonal food (01962-853834, 11am-11pm, £-££).

Military Quarter

Winchester College Chapel

Winchester College

One of the UK's most illustrious public schools, Winchester College is one of the oldest continuously running schools in the country, founded in 1382 by William of Wykeham, Bishop of Winchester (1366-1404). You can take a guided tour of the school buildings and the **Treasury Museum**, a 14th-century stable block housing the College's treasures.

Church, parts of which date from the 12th century, and is home to the amateur Winchester Dramatic Society. The **Winchester Discovery Centre** is a world-class venue for creativity, learning and culture, and houses the main library, public galleries and a 180-seat theatre, which stages gigs, concerts, talks, shows and exhibitions.

Winchester is surrounded by green spaces, notably the **South Downs National Park**, although the city itself has relatively few parks and gardens. One exception is beautiful **Abbey (Mill) Gardens**, part of the site of St Mary's Abbey, once one of the largest religious houses in England. The gardens encompass the Mayor of Winchester's official residence (Abbey House) and the original Abbey Mill. To the north of the city is **Winnall Moors Nature Reserve**, which is criss-crossed by the River Itchen and includes a wide range of habitats.

When you're peckish, Winchester has a surfeit of excellent restaurants, cafés and pubs, catering for every taste and budget, and if shopping's your bag, then **Winchester Market** (Wed-Sat) is a must, not to mention the city's profusion of independent stores and household names.

Abbey Mill

Great Minster Street

Windsor

Address: Windsor, Berks SL4 1QF (windsor.gov.uk)

Rail: from 31min via Paddington and Waterloo stations

Road: 50min (25mi) via M4

Nearby: Cookham, Eton, **Legoland**

A historic market town on the River Thames in Berkshire, 25 miles west of London, Windsor is world-famous as the site of majestic Windsor Castle, one of the official residences of the British royal family. The river forms the boundary with neighbouring Eton, with its celebrated public school. Three miles southeast of Windsor is the village of Old Windsor – once the site of an important Anglo-Saxon palace – which predates Windsor by some 300 years.

The early history of Windsor is unknown, but it was believed to have been settled before 1070, when William the Conqueror constructed the first timber motte and bailey castle (the stone walls weren't built until 1173-79). Today, magnificent **Windsor Castle** (fee, see box) – covering 13 acres, it's the largest and oldest occupied castle in the world – dominates the skyline for miles around. Since its foundation, the castle has been extensively remodelled and enlarged by subsequent monarchs. Today's castle is, in essence, a Georgian and Victorian design based on a medieval structure, with Gothic features reinvented in a modern style.

St George's Chapel

Other buildings of note in Windsor include the parish **Church of St John the Baptist** in the High Street; dating from 1822, it replaced an ancient church with Saxon and Norman detailing. In the west gallery is a famous painting of *The Last Supper* by German artist

Windsor Castle

Queen's Drawing Room, Windsor Castle

Francis de Cleyn, court painter to James I. Nearby is **Windsor Guildhall,** designed by Sir Thomas Fitch in 1687 and completed by Sir Christopher Wren. It's home to the **Windsor & Royal Borough Museum** (fee) on the ground floor, which relates the history of the town and its people. Windsor contains a host of handsome listed buildings dating from the 16th-19th centuries, including the **Theatre Royal** (see below), hotels, pubs, shops and private dwellings, including the 16th-century **Crooked House of Windsor** (1687) on the High Street next to Queen Charlotte Street; just 51ft long, it's the shortest street in Britain. Half a mile south of Windsor Castle (in Home Park) is grand **Frogmore House,** built in 1680-4 by Charles II and subsequently occupied by a succession of royal residents (nearby Frogmore Cottage

is now home to the Duke & Duchess of Sussex). The opulent gardens (fee, restricted opening) were laid out in the 1790s and contain the Royal Mausoleum, the burial site of Queen Victoria and Prince Albert.

Crooked House

Across the river, historic Eton is a pretty little town, quieter than Windsor, and well worth a visit. The town is dominated by the world-famous public school, **Eton College,** founded by Henry VI in 1440 to provide free education to 70 poor boys who would go on to study at King's College, Cambridge, which he founded in 1441. Today, it's an independent boarding school and sixth form for boys and the most prestigious private school in the world; some 20 British Prime Ministers and generations of royalty and aristocracy (British and foreign) were educated at Eton.

Windsor Castle Tours

Public tours take in the castle precincts, the Round Tower, St George's Chapel, the State Apartments (with opulent furnishings and paintings from the royal art collection) and Queen Mary's famous Dolls' House (see rct.uk/visit/windsor-castle for info).

When it comes to green spaces, Windsor has glorious **Home Park** on its doorstep, a 655-acre royal park on the eastern side of Windsor Castle administered by the Crown Estate. The park – which is divided from the main Windsor Great Park (4,800 acres) by Albert Road (A308) – was part of the private grounds of Windsor Castle until 1851, when Queen Victoria decreed that it be used for public recreation. Along with beautiful open parkland, gardens and avenues of fine trees, the park contains farmland, a golf course, playing fields and various sports facilities. Other smaller parks in Windsor include attractive **Alexandra Gardens** alongside the river, which hosts an ice rink in winter; **Bachelor's Acre,** a charming small park with a water feature; and **The Brocas,** an expansive meadow in Eton, providing great views of the castle.

Home Park

Food & Drink

- **Browns Windsor:** Bar and brasserie on the Promenade with lovely views, serving tasty British food (01753-831976, 9am-midnight, Sun 9am-10pm, £-££).
- **Cinnamon Café:** Intimate café serving excellent coffee/tea and a wide variety of cakes and savoury dishes (7am-6pm, £).
- **The Duchess of Cambridge:** Welcoming Victorian pub adjacent to the castle, with a cosy bar and terrace serving creative British grub and award-winning ales (01753-864405, 10/11am-10.30pm/midnight, £).

Nearby Eton College is home to three museums (Sun 2.30-5pm, free) – the **Museum of Eton Life,** the **Natural History Museum** and **Eton Museum of Antiquities** – while in Eton Wick is the **History on Wheels Museum** (fee). Entertainment in Windsor includes the **Old Court,** a vibrant arts centre featuring an eclectic mix of live music, drama, comedy and film, while the **Old Ticket Hall** is Windsor's best live music venue. If drama is your thing, the intimate Edwardian **Theatre Royal** offers a wide-ranging repertoire, from classics and pantomime to first-run drama productions.

When you need to refuel, Windsor has an abundance of eating and drinking establishments, from fast food to fine dining, gastro pubs to ritzy bars. Shoppers are well catered for, too, with independent shops, arcades such as historic **Windsor Royal Station** – located in a former Victorian railway station – and popular street food and farmers' markets.

Eton College

Willy Lott's Cottage, East Bergholt, Suffolk (see page 74)

2.
Villages

This chapter features ten historic villages, most of which are accessible from London in less that 90 minutes (many less than an hour) by train. They include the charming villages of Alfriston and Bosham in Sussex; the National Trust Tudor village of Chiddingstone in Kent; medieval Coggeshall in Essex and Lavenham in Suffolk; picturesque Cookham on the Thames in Berkshire; East Bergholt (birthplace of John Constable) in Suffolk; and Great Missenden in the Chilterns, former home of children's author Roald Dahl.

Alfriston

Address: Alfriston, East Sussex BN26 5TL
(alfriston-village.co.uk)

Rail: from 1h 7min to Lewes via Victoria station,
then 125 bus (ca. 15min)

Road: 2h (66mi) via M23/A23

Nearby: Charleston, Drusillas Park, **Eastbourne**,
Herstmonceux Castle, Pevensey, South Downs
National Park

Alfriston Clergy House

Nestled within the South Downs National Park, charming Alfriston in East Sussex (66 miles from London) is one of England's most beautiful villages. Dating back to Saxon times, when it was recorded as *Aelfrictun* (the town of Alfric), it's one of the country's best-preserved medieval villages and has a host of timber-framed buildings, many dating from the 14th century.

To the east of the village is the River Cuckmere and alongside it the village green, called the Tye. In the centre is **St Andrew's Church**, which has Saxon origins, although most of the current building dates from the 14th century. This beautiful building dubbed 'the cathedral of the South Downs' due to its impressive size – is built in a cruciform shape topped by a central tower and slender spire. Close by is **Alfriston Clergy House**, originally the village vicarage, which was the first property to be acquired by the National Trust (in 1896 for £10). Grade II* listed, it's a classic example of a 14th-century Wealden hall house with a thatched roof, timber-framed walls and a lovely riverside garden. Also on the Tye is the handsome **Alfriston War Memorial Hall** (now the village hall) and the **Old Chapel Centre**, a former Georgian non-conformist (Unitarian) chapel built in 1801, now a popular wedding venue.

After exploring the village, take a stroll along the banks of the Cuckmere or up onto

St Andrew's Church

the Downs – the South Downs Way crosses the river in the centre of the village – to soak up the area's peace and tranquillity. Further afield is Drusillas Park, a 10-acre zoo a few miles north of the village, while four miles south is the delightful coastal town of Seaford.

Inspired by the beauty of Alfriston, Eleanor Farjeon wrote the popular hymn *Morning Has Broken* in 1931; it was a hit for Cat Stevens in the '70s.

If you fancy staying overnight, the village has many fine hotels, inns and bed & breakfast establishments, including Chestnuts B&B, Deans Place Hotel, the George Inn, the Smugglers Inn, the Star Inn, Wingrove House and Ye Olde Smugglers Inn. When you're peckish the village has a number of restaurants and cafés, along with the George, Smugglers and Star inns that have been welcoming travellers for centuries. Alfriston also has many interesting shops and boutiques, and hosts events throughout the year including theatrical spectacles, music festivals and traditional fetes.

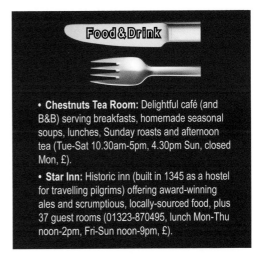

Food & Drink

- **Chestnuts Tea Room:** Delightful café (and B&B) serving breakfasts, homemade seasonal soups, lunches, Sunday roasts and afternoon tea (Tue-Sat 10.30am-5pm, 4.30pm Sun, closed Mon, £).

- **Star Inn:** Historic inn (built in 1345 as a hostel for travelling pilgrims) offering award-winning ales and scrumptious, locally-sourced food, plus 37 guest rooms (01323-870495, lunch Mon-Thu noon-2pm, Fri-Sun noon-9pm, £).

High Street & George Inn

Bosham

Holy Trinity Church

One of the prettiest villages on the south coast, Bosham (pronounced 'Bozzam') in West Sussex (75 miles from London) enjoys a delightful setting on a small peninsula between two tidal creeks at the eastern end of Chichester Harbour. The village – a popular sailing centre – has an enchanting olde-worlde feel, where charming 17th- and 18th-century buildings line the narrow, winding streets and alleys leading to the harbour.

Historically Bosham is one of the most significant villages in Sussex. It was from Bosham that King Harold II (1022-1066) – the last crowned Anglo-Saxon king of England – sailed in 1064 to negotiate with William of Normandy, a voyage that led to William the Conqueror's fateful (for Harold) return in 1066. Both Harold and Bosham's Saxon church are shown on the Bayeux Tapestry, while the *Domesday Book* of 1086 lists Bosham as one of the wealthiest manors in England. King Canute (Cnut) was said to have lived in Bosham and legend has it that it was here that he ordered the waves to retreat.

Christians have worshipped here for well over 1,000 years; according to the Venerable Bede, Bosham was one of the first sites in Sussex to be visited by St Wilfrid who preached here around AD681. **Holy Trinity Church** (Grade I listed) dates back to Saxon times and the lower stages of the tower and the first third of the chancel

Bosham Panorama

Food & Drink

• **Anchor Bleu:** Historic harbourside pub, serving good food and a wide range of ales (01243-573956, lunch Mon-Fri noon-2.30pm, Sat-Sun noon-3/4pm, £).

• **Marwick's:** Part of the Millstream Hotel & Restaurant, Marwick's brasserie has a nice alfresco courtyard area, serving British favourites (01243-573234, lunch noon-2pm, £).

many more species, and offers lovely walks along the sea shore. You can stroll around the harbour and quay and watch the sailing boats, but be careful where you park as during spring tides the road that runs along the harbour is inundated!

If you're tempted to stay longer, Bosham offers a range of accommodation and a variety of pubs, restaurants and tea rooms, where you can enjoy everything from an espresso to a gourmet meal. Other diversions include Bosham Walk, a popular arcade of artisan arts and crafts shops, and Bosham Gallery, while nearby Chichester (see page 25) offers a wealth of attractions.

survive from this period. The chancel arch was built in the 11th century shortly after the Norman Conquest, the crypt is 14th century, while the unusual shingled spire dates from the 15th century. The religious theme continues at the **Hamblin Centre**, a spiritual sanctuary set in the grounds of the former home of Henry Thomas Hamblin, a Christian mystic and prolific author who lived in Bosham from 1914 until his death in 1958.

The Bosham area has been inhabited since Roman times – it's close to the famous Roman palace at **Fishbourne** (fee) – and several important Roman buildings have been found in northern Bosham around Broadbridge.

To the south, Chichester harbour is a wetland and bird sanctuary of international importance for migrating wildfowl, shelduck, wigeon, Brent geese, waders and

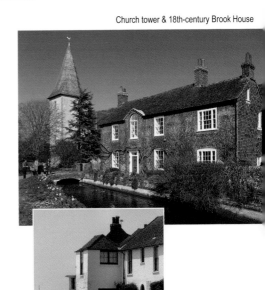

Church tower & 18th-century Brook House

High tide

Chiddingstone

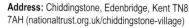

Address: Chiddingstone, Edenbridge, Kent TN8 7AH (nationaltrust.org.uk/chiddingstone-village)

Rail: from 41min to Tonbridge via Charing Cross, then train to Chiddingstone Causeway and bus/taxi to village (3mi)

Road: 1h 15min (45mi) via A13 and M25

Nearby: Hever Castle, Penshurst Place, Tonbridge

Food & Drink

- **Castle Inn:** Charming historic inn dating from 1420, offering tasty food and fine ales from local Larkins Brewery (01892-870371, lunch noon-3pm, £).

- **Tulip Tree Tea Rooms:** Cosy café for breakfast, lunch or afternoon tea, with log burner and outside seating in summer (10am-5pm, £).

Located in Kent on the River Eden just 45 miles from London, Chiddingstone is the best-preserved one-street Tudor village in England, and very popular with film crews. The parish dates from Anglo-Saxon times and was given to Bishop Odo in 1072 as part of his Earldom of Kent, noted in the *Domesday Book* of 1086. The village has been owned by the National Trust since 1939, including the **Castle Inn**, houses, school and post office (everything but the castle and church).

The striking architecture is typical of the Kent style, with half-timbered sides, gables and stone-hung red-tiled roofs, coupled with a narrow main street and cobbled pavements. The **Post Office** building dates to at least 1453 and was once owned by Thomas Boleyn, Anne Boleyn's father, while the 13th-century parish church of **St Mary the Virgin** was largely rebuilt in the 14th century and its fine west tower (with its stair turret and four pinnacles) was added in the 15th century. A lightning strike in 1624 destroyed all but the tower and the church was rebuilt and rededicated in 1629.

The history of **Chiddingstone Castle** goes back to the early 16th century, when the original Tudor dwelling was built; this was replaced in the 1670s by High Street House, which in turn was transformed into a mock medieval castle in the 1800s. It's now a museum (open April-Oct Sun-Wed, fee) containing the collection of over 4,000 objects amassed by

Post Office

Chiddingstone Castle

The Chiding Stone

The stone after which the village is thought to be named is a sandstone rock formation dating back millions of years that's enshrouded in myth and folklore. It's variously thought to be a druid altar, an ancient Anglo-Saxon boundary marker, and a place of punishment for nagging wives and wilful daughters!

former owner Denys Eyre Bower, including Japanese lacquer, Samurai armour and swords, ancient Egyptian antiquities, Royal Stuart portraits, Jacobite memorabilia and Buddhist artefacts. The castle also has 35 acres of beautiful informal grounds, including a lake, woodland, herbaceous borders, a courtyard rose garden and Victorian orangery.

While here it's worth visiting **Hever Castle** and its beautiful gardens, just 3½ miles to the west – an easy hour's walk on lanes and paths, through fields and woods. A handsome 13th-century manor house – the home of the Sidney family since 1552 – the castle was the childhood home of Anne Boleyn, second wife of Henry VIII. Also within a few miles is glorious **Penshurst Place**, a 14th-century manor house with splendid gardens.

Hever Castle

Penshurst Place

Chilham

Address: Chilham, Kent CT4 8DE (enjoychilham. com).

Rail: from 38min to Ashford International via St Pancras, Charing Cross or Victoria, then bus (15m)

Road: 1h 30min (64mi) via A2 and M2

Nearby: Canterbury, **Faversham**, Kent Downs AONB, **Whitstable**

St Mary's

Just off the Square is the 13th-century parish church of **St Mary's**, built largely in English Perpendicular style, replacing a Saxon building dating from the 7th century. The tower was built in 1534 and houses a belfry with six bells and a clock, the latter installed in 1727. The church contains a number of fine funerary monuments, including one to Lady Mary Digges (d. 1631), wife of Jacobean diplomat Sir Dudley Digges (1583-1639). The striking memorial is composed of four seated statues representing cardinal virtues around a central column.

Overlooking the beautiful Great Stour River valley, 64 miles southeast of London and 6 miles from Canterbury, historic Chilham is a charming picture-postcard village in Kent. The elegant village square is bounded by delightful medieval and Jacobean half-timbered buildings. Much of the village is a heritage conservation area, making it a popular film and TV location – *Poirot*, *Miss Marple* and *Emma* have been filmed here. Among the finest buildings are the half-timbered **Tudor Lodge** (dating from 1370-1410), **Tudor Cottage**, and the **White Horse Inn** – all located in the Square – while **Cumberland House** (1470-1510), **Orions Cottage**, and **Burgoyne** (1450-1480) are on the Street. A short walk west of the village centre is **Chilham Village Hall**, which occupies a 15th-century tithe barn.

At the other end of the Square is **Chilham Castle** which is, in fact, two castles. The original polygonal Norman keep – built for Henry II – dates from 1174 and is still inhabited, making it one of the oldest occupied dwellings in Britain. Next to it is a Jacobean castle/manor house built in 1616 by Sir Dudley Digges on a hexagonal plan – lovingly restored by the current owners – with sweeping views of the

Chilham Square

Shelly's Tea Rooms

surrounding area. The gateway to Chilham Park (1616) was built by Inigo Jones, while the estate's beautiful landscaped gardens were designed by Thomas Heron and Lancelot 'Capability' Brown. The gardens are open to the public on Tuesdays (Jun-Sep), while historical tours of the house are possible by special arrangement (see chilham-castle.co.uk). The estate plays host to a number of events throughout the year, including open-air performances from the touring Shakespeare's Globe Theatre Company.

The village is home to two historic public houses, the 14th-century White Horse and the 15th-century Woolpack, while other amenities include a restaurant and tea shop, post office, gift shop, tennis club, sports centre and children's playground. When you've exhausted the village's delights, the surrounding Kent Downs countryside is criss-crossed by footpaths, bridleways and country lanes, while the North Downs Way and the Pilgrims' Way to Canterbury go right through the centre of the village.

Chilham Castle

Coggeshall

i

Address: Coggeshall, Essex CO6 1TS

Rail: from 1h 8min to Braintree or Marks Tey via Liverpool Street station, then 70 bus (15min)

Road: 1h 20min (60mi) via M11 & A120

Nearby: Braintree, **Colchester**

The market 'town' of Coggeshall – one of the most beautiful and historic in Essex – lies on the River Blackwater, 60 miles northeast of London. Although it's the size of a small town with over 4,500 residents, locals insist it's a village and it has won

many awards in this category, hence its inclusion here. It dates back at least to early Saxon times, and there's

Food & Drink

• **Clock House Café & Bar:** Cosy café/restaurant beneath the town's iconic clock, the Clock House's garden is the perfect spot for lunch (10am-5pm, 11pm Thu-Sat, closed Mon, £).

• **White Hart:** A 15th-century inn with 20 rooms, the White Hart is a great place to enjoy classic pub grub (01376-561654, 7/8am-11pm, £).

also evidence of Roman settlement – the town straddles the ancient Roman road of Stane Street which linked Colchester and Braintree.

Coggeshall prospered during the Middle Ages, thanks to its thriving wool and cloth trade and, subsequently, its silk and velvet weaving, lace-making and brewing industries. Today, its affluent past is reflected in streets of wonky, timber-framed buildings, some built as early as the 1300s. These include the handsome wool church of **St Peter ad Vincula**, constructed in the Perpendicular style in the 15th century and one of the largest churches in Essex. Other notable buildings include **Paycocke's House** (National Trust, fee), built around 1500 for wealthy clothier Thomas Paycocke; its handsome carved ceiling beams are testament to the wealth generated by the wool cloth trade in the 16th century.

Among the town's abundance of ancient buildings are 16th-century **Chapel Inn** in the market place and timber-framed **White Hart Inn** on West Street, parts of which date from the 1400s. The latter was originally

Clock Tower, Stoneham Street

Grange Barn

Across the river on Bridge Street is the impressive **Grange Barn** (fee), one of Europe's oldest timber-framed buildings, constructed in the 13th century by the Cistercians of Coggeshall Abbey and now owned (as is Paycocke's House) by the National Trust. The abbey was founded even earlier, in 1140, and some of its former monastic buildings still exist and form part of the Abbey Estate Livery on the banks of the Blackwater at the end of Abbey Lane. Nearby is **St Nicholas's Chapel** (1220), the abbey's former gate house.

owned by one Thomas Hawkes, who was burned at the stake at Vicarage Field during the reign of Queen Mary. On Church Street, next to St Peter ad Vincula, is the **Woolpack Inn**, built in 1408, while beside Paycocke's

House is the former 16th-century **Fleece Inn**, opposite which is the **Sir Robert Hitcham School**, established in 1636 (it now houses a vet's surgery). Near to Chapel Inn is the iconic, weather-boarded, blue and white **Clock Tower**, built in 1887, although the building dates from the 14th century.

To learn more about the town's fascinating history, visit **Coggeshall Museum** (open April-Sept, Sun 2.15-4.45pm, free) on Stoneham Street, next to the village hall. When you've toured the town's sites – an excellent leaflet is published by the museum entitled *A Walk around Coggeshall* – enjoy a break in one of the town's many historic inns or a little retail therapy at Coggeshall's market (Thu), established by royal charter in 1256.

Paycocke's House & Garden (front & rear)

Cookham

> **Address:** Cookham, Berks SL6 9SF (cookham.com)
>
> **Rail:** from 55min via Paddington, change at Maidenhead
>
> **Road:** 55min (30mi) via M4
>
> **Nearby:** Bekonscot, Bray, Cliveden, Maidenhead, Marlow, Windsor

Holy Trinity Church

A historic and affluent village on the Thames in Berkshire, 30 miles west of London, charming Cookham is a delightful day-trip destination. The parish includes three villages – Cookham, Cookham Dean (noted for its cherry orchards) and Cookham Rise – known collectively as 'The Cookhams'. The area has been inhabited for thousands of years (prehistoric burial mounds have been found nearby) and the Roman road of Camlet Way is believed to have crossed the Thames at nearby Sashes Island on its way to St Albans and Silchester. The village is thought to have grown up around an 8th-century Anglo-Saxon abbey, while Cookham is recorded in the *Domesday Book* of 1086 as *Cocheham*.

The village contains a wealth of listed buildings, including the **Bel & the Dragon** inn, which dates from 1417 and is one of the earliest licensed houses in England. However, Cookham's oldest building is handsome **Holy Trinity Church**, built in the late 12th century, which although much altered over the

Sir Stanley Spencer

Cookham is perhaps best-known today as the former home of artist Sir Stanley Spencer (1891-1959), who lived here for most of his life and painted many of the village's features. He's remembered by the superb **Stanley Spencer Gallery** (fee), based in the former Methodist chapel, which contains a permanent display of his works.

River Thames from the Ferry pub

Food & Drink

• **The Ferry:** Stylish upscale pub/restaurant on the river with a terrace, serving modern British fare (good value set lunch) and fine ales (01628-525123, 11am-10.30pm/midnight, £-££).

• **Teapot Tea Shop:** Shabby chic café on the High Street serving excellent coffee, tea, cakes and light lunches (10am-5pm, £).

centuries still contains some Norman features. In its early days it housed an anchoress (a female religious hermit) who was allegedly bricked into her cell for 12 years to pray for Henry II – he paid her a halfpenny a day for her travails. In the Middle Ages, most of Cookham was owned by Cirencester Abbey and the timber-framed **Church Gate House** (ca. 1350) near the church was reportedly the abbot's residence. More recently, Holy Trinity's churchyard was the setting for Sir Stanley Spencer's seminal painting, *The Resurrection, Cookham*, completed in 1927.

A visit to Cookham wouldn't be complete without seeing handsome **Cliveden House** (fee), 2½ miles to the east across the Thames. Cliveden is famous for its magnificent 375 acres of gardens and woodlands, maze and superb sculpture collection – and for being the place where John Profumo began his ill-fated affair with Christine Keeler. The Italianate mansion – designed by Charles Barry and built in 1851 – is now a private luxury hotel, but guided tours are available (see nationaltrust.org.uk/cliveden).

When you're peckish, Cookham offers a surfeit of superb restaurants and historic inns, and if you fancy a stroll after lunch, the area is noted for its abundance of signposted walks. A stroll along the river, from where Kenneth Grahame is said to have drawn inspiration for *Wind in the Willows*, is an especially tranquil treat.

Cliveden House

East Bergholt

Address: East Bergholt, Suffolk CO7 6RA
(eastbergholt.org)

Rail: from 55min to Manningtree via Liverpool
Street station, then bus/taxi (4 miles)

Road: 1h 30min (76mi) via A12

Nearby: Colchester, Dedham, Dedham Vale
AONB, **Lavenham**, Stour Estuary

Food & Drink

• **Carriers Arms:** Family-run pub and restaurant
in a historic 14/15th-century building, offering
home-cooked food and fine ales (01206-298392,
lunch noon-2.15pm, £).

• **Oranges & Lemons:** Award-winning café and
craft shop occupying the former King's Head pub,
serving irresistible cakes (10am-5pm, 9am Sat,
closed Mon, £).

Bucolic East Bergholt in Suffolk (76 miles from
London) is a sizeable village on the north bank of the
River Stour in the heart of what's known as 'Constable
Country', the area comprising East Bergholt, Dedham
and Flatford. The village is home to a number of large,
elegant houses, many built by wool merchants who
made huge fortunes in the Stour Valley in the 13th-16th
centuries. These include **Stour House**, once the home
of Randolph Churchill, the only son of Sir Winston
Churchill; **Lambe School**, founded by Edward Lambe
in 1594 and now the village hall; and **East Bergholt
Place**, which has a celebrated garden and arboretum

(fee), created by Charles Cuthbert Eley and his son, Sir
Geoffrey Eley.

The oldest building in the village is **St Mary's Church**,
which dates from around 1350 and is built in late
Perpendicular style. Unusually, it has no tower or spire
to house its bells. A tower was planned but was never
completed and in 1531 a wooden bell cage was erected
in the churchyard in which the bells are housed upside
down. The bells are thought to be the heaviest five bells
still rung in England, and are pushed by hand rather

St Mary's Church

Willy Lott's Cottage

East Bergholt is celebrated as the birthplace of artist John Constable (1776-1837), England's greatest landscape artist, whose wealthy father owned nearby **Flatford Mill** (free). The mill – now owned by the National Trust – is a short stroll south of the village along a country lane and was the location for one of Constable's best-known paintings, *The Hay Wain*, which depicted **Willy Lott's Cottage**. Nearby is 16th-century **Flatford Bridge Cottage** (also painted by Constable), which houses an exhibition about the artist, and the **RSPB Flatford Wildlife Garden**.

than pulled by a rope. The church's spectacular interior is well worth a look. The nearby **Old Hall** (with over 100 rooms and 70 acres of land) is a 16th-century manor house that's been home to a Benedictine nunnery, an army barracks and a Franciscan friary. It now houses the Old Hall Community, a single household of some 50 people who live co-operatively and farm organically.

From Flatford you can follow in Constable's footsteps along the Stour to the nearby town of Dedham, where he attended school. Dedham was the birthplace of another eminent artist, Sir Alfred Munnings (1878-1959), and is now a showcase for local artists – it's home to the **Munnings Art Museum**, the **Dedham Art & Craft Centre** and the handsome **Shakespeare House Gallery**. A small electric passenger boat runs along the Stour between Stratford St Mary, Dedham, Flatford and Brantham between April and October.

The area has a good selection of inns and restaurants – indeed, East Bergholt has more pubs than any other village in Suffolk. If you fancy a walk, Dedham Vale is designated an Area of Outstanding Natural Beauty, while the nearby Stour Estuary is an RSPB nature reserve.

Flatford Mill

Great Missenden

Address: Great Missenden, Bucks HO16 0AL (visitchilterns.co.uk/market-towns/great-missenden.html)

Rail: from 41min via Marylebone station

Road: 1h 5min (35mi) via A40

Nearby: Amersham, Aylesbury, **The Chilterns AONB**, High Wycombe, Hughenden Manor, **Waddesdon Manor**

Quaint, charming and effortlessly affluent, Great Missenden is tucked away in the Misbourne Valley in Buckinghamshire, 35 miles northwest of London, in the heart of the Chiltern Hills. It was established in the late Middle Ages as a major stop on the coaching route between London and the Midlands, and now attracts wealthy commuters who can afford to put down roots in one of Britain's richest villages. The centre is a riot of

Crown House

Red Pump Garage

higgledy-piggledy streets and cobbled alleys, brightly-painted front doors and hanging baskets, complete with a medieval parish church, **St Peter & St Paul**, which dates back to the 14th century.

The village is synonomous with children's author Roald Dahl (1916-1990), who lived in Great Missenden from 1954 until his death in 1990. His home (and workplace) was an 18th-century farmhouse called **Gipsy House** on Whitefield Lane, complete with maze, bird house and a gypsy caravan Dahl's children used to play in, which inspired the one in which Danny lived in *Danny, The Champion of the World*. Several High Street locations found their way into Dahl's books, including timber-framed **Crown House** (number 70), the location of Sophie's 'norphanage' in the *Big Friendly Giant* (BFG), and the **Red Pump Garage** petrol station (number 66A), with its '50s-style pumps and white Shell Oil sign at the top, the inspiration for the garage in *Danny*. Dahl is buried at St Peter & St Paul, and his grave is a pilgrimage site for children who

Gipsy House

Roald Dahl

When you need to refuel, the village has a wide selection of pubs, restaurants and cafés although, sadly, no chocolate factory.

Food & Drink

- **The Cross Keys:** Historic 16th-century pub, offering good food and ales (01494-865373, 11am-11pm/midnight, £-££).

- **Roald Dahl Museum Café:** Child-friendly menu with soups, 'sandwitches' and a 'splendiferous' afternoon tea (Tue-Sat 9am-5pm, Sun 10am-5pm, closed Mon, £).

Big Friendly Giant

leave toys and flowers at his grave (follow the BFG's footprints to find it).

Gipsy House is still owned by the Dahl family and closed to the public, but you can discover more about the man at the **Roald Dahl Museum & Story Centre** (fee). Opened in 2005 in an old coaching inn and yard on the High Street, it tells the story of Dahl's life and work, with hands-on activities for young visitors. Also on the High Street is **Missenden Abbey**, a country house (now a conference centre) built in 1574 on the site of the original Augustinian abbey, which was founded in 1133 and dissolved in 1538 by Henry VIII.

The **Chilterns** surrounding the village are a superb walking and cycling area with an abundance of trails. You can follow the Misbourne Stream and link back to the village through the Chilterns' woodlands and farmland, or visit the charming satellite villages of Little Missenden (2.8 miles) and The Lee (3.4 miles), the location for the very first episode of *Midsomer Murders*.

Hughenden Manor

Five miles south of Great Missenden is **Hughenden Manor**, former country home of Victorian Prime Minister Benjamin Disraeli (1804-1881). It's now owned by the National Trust, and offers a vivid and entertaining insight into Disraeli's colourful personal and political life. The formal garden has been recreated, based on the original designs, and there are woodland walks through the rolling parkland.

Lavenham

Address: Lavenham, Suffolk CO10 9SA (visit-lavenham.co.uk)

Rail: from 1h 19min to Sudbury (change at Marks Tey) via Liverpool Street station, then 753/754 bus (30m)

Road: 1h 50min (76mi) via M11

Nearby: Bury St Edmunds, **East Bergholt**, Long Melford, Sudbury

Food & Drink

• **Cock Horse Inn:** Friendly traditional pub on Church Street serving locally-sourced food and cask ales (01787-827330, Tue-Sun 11am-11pm/midnight, 6pm Sun, closed Mon, £).

• **Lavenham Blue Vintage Tea Rooms:** Timber-framed 16th-century cottage with courtyard patio on Market Square, serving delicious cakes, lunches and afternoon tea (10am-4.30pm, closed Thu, £).

A historic market town in Suffolk, 76 miles from London, Lavenham is quite possibly the finest medieval village in England. A significant settlement since Anglo-Saxon times, following the Norman Conquest the village passed to Aubrey de Vere I, whose family held the estate until 1604. It was awarded its market charter from Henry III in 1257 and grew to become one of England's wealthiest wool villages during the Middle Ages. It still has all the hallmarks of prosperous medieval England, with its streets of colourful, crooked, half-timbered houses, many immaculately preserved, which include over 300 listed buildings.

First stop on the Market Square is the fine **Guildhall of Corpus Christi** (National Trust, fee). This is one of the most spectacular 16th-century (1529) timber-framed buildings in the country and has fascinating exhibits on the history of Lavenham and its wool trade. The nearby saffron-hued **Little Hall** (fee) was built in the 1390s for the Causton family, and is now a museum providing a unique timeline of Lavenham's architectural and cultural history; it also has a delightful knot and rose garden.

On Water Street, **De Vere House** may look familiar; this 14th-century cottage was the birthplace of Harry Potter in the Deathly Hallows films. Just up the road is the **Lavenham Wool Hall**, completed in

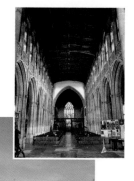

St Peter & St Paul

1464, while nearby is 13th-century **Lavenham Priory** (now a hotel) and just around the corner in Barn Street is the **Old Grammar School** (1647) where artist John Constable was a pupil.

> Lavenham is a living film set and has been a backdrop for many movies, from cult '60s horror flick *Witchfinder General* to *Harry Potter and the Deathly Hallows*.

The town's prosperity – by the 15th century, Lavenham was paying more in taxes than Lincoln and York! – is best illustrated by the lavish parish wool church of **St Peter & St Paul** (1485-1525), one of the finest examples of Late Perpendicular Gothic architecture in England. Located on a hill at the top of the High Street, the cathedral-like church is vast for a village congregation, and its 141ft tower lays claim to being the highest village church tower in Britain. Just north of the church, the **Lavenham Hall Gallery** with its 7-acre sculpture garden is well worth a visit. There are many galleries in Lavenham – check out the truly twisted **Crooked House** on the High Street – and a wide choice of places to eat.

Further afield, the village of Long Melford (5 miles away) is home to two splendid stately homes: 14th-century **Kentwell Hall** and 16th-century **Melford Hall**, which both hosted Elizabeth I. Or head to Sudbury (7 miles) to see stunning **Gainsborough's House**, birthplace of one of England's finest artists, Thomas Gainsborough (1727-1788), now a museum and gallery with a glorious garden and venerable mulberry tree.

Lavenham Houses

Shere

Address: Shere, Surrey GU5 9HF (sheredelight.com)

Rail: from 1h 3min to Gomshall (1 mile, change at Guildford) via Waterloo or Blackfriars station

Road: 1h 10min (35mi) via A3

Nearby: Dorking, Guildford, Surrey Hills AONB, **Watts Gallery & Artists' Village**

Charming Shere is popular with filmmakers and has starred in many films, including *Bridget Jones: The Edge of Reason*, *Foyle's War* and *Four Weddings and a Funeral*.

A beautiful, quintessential English village, Shere in Surrey is 35 miles south of London, nestled firmly in the Surrey Hills on the River Tillingbourne. The village dates from the Anglo-Saxon period and appears in the *Domesday Book* of 1086 as Essira and Essire in the ancient hundred of Blackheath, held by William the Conqueror. **Shere Manor Estate** is a privately-owned estate that has been in the Bray family – the Lords of the Manor – since being granted to Sir Reginald Bray by Henry VII in the late 15th century.

This unspoilt village has grown around a central cluster of old timber-framed houses – many dating from the 16th and 17th centuries – and has all the small village essentials, such as a blacksmith, tea room, art gallery, cricket pitch, pub and Norman church. There are 30 listed buildings, including St James's Church and the idyllic 15th-century **White Horse Inn**, where Jude Law romanced Cameron Diaz in *The Holiday*. Lower Street, which runs alongside the River Tillingbourne to the ford, has the Old Forge, the Old Prison, Weavers House and Wheelwright Cottage, while Middle Street still contains a working forge. **East**

St James's Church

Lodge, aka Manor House Lodge, at the eastern end of Upper Street is a much later building, designed by (Sir) Edwin Lutyens and built in 1894 for Sir Reginald Bray as a gatehouse to Shere Manor. Lutyens also designed the Western Cottages in Upper Street and the building that houses the Dabbling Duck café on Middle Street.

The oldest building in the village is 12th-century **St James's Church** (1190), designed

White Horse Inn

in the Early English Transitional style, with 13th-14th century additions, which replaced an earlier Anglo-Saxon church. It contains a tiny enclosed cell in which Christine Carpenter, an anchoress (religious recluse) lived from 1329 to 1332, her only contact with the outside world being via a grid and an aperture through which food was passed. The church contains an alms chest dating from 1200, several brass plaques in the chancel dating from 1412, and a 14th-century quatrefoil window and squint. **Shere Museum** (free) offers an interesting insight into the history of the village and surrounding area.

A visit to Shere wouldn't be complete without a stroll in the beautiful surrounding **Surrey Hills** Area of Outstanding Natural Beauty (AONB), designated in 1958, which covers a quarter of the county of Surrey (163mi²). This bucolic landscape – once the haunt of smugglers and sheep stealers – features numerous trails and paths from Shere, including the Shere Trail (3mi), a gentle path west to Albury and back, following the course of the Tillingbourne, taking in historic churches, ancient houses and river features along the way.

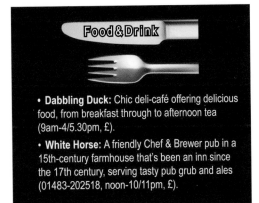

Food & Drink

- **Dabbling Duck:** Chic deli-café offering delicious food, from breakfast through to afternoon tea (9am-4/5.30pm, £).
- **White Horse:** A friendly Chef & Brewer pub in a 15th-century farmhouse that's been an inn since the 17th century, serving tasty pub grub and ales (01483-202518, noon-10/11pm, £).

East Lodge

Dabbling Duck & Old Forge

Old Prison

Eastbourne, West Sussex (see page 88)

3.
Coastal Resorts

Many seaside resorts are accessible for day trips from London. Those featured below include some of England's most popular coastal resorts (many with historic piers), all less than 90 minutes from London by direct train. They include ever-popular Brighton in West Sussex; picturesque Deal and the celebrated historic resorts of Margate and Ramsgate in Kent; the ancient town of Hastings (and nearby Battle) in East Sussex; fashionable Eastbourne and Worthing in West Sussex; and the charming fishing village of Whitstable in Kent.

Brighton

Address: Brighton, West Sussex BN2 1TW
(visitbrighton.com)

Rail: from 1h 11min via Blackfriars, London Bridge,
St Pancras and Victoria stations

Road: 1h 55min (54mi) via M23/A23

Nearby: Eastbourne, Lewes, **Worthing**

Located in West Sussex on the south coast, 54 miles from London, bohemian Brighton (part of the city of Brighton & Hove) is one of the UK's most popular seaside resorts. It's renowned for its quirky shopping areas, diverse culture, vibrant music and arts scene, and large LGBT population (it's the unofficial 'gay capital of the UK'). The town's origins date back to the Neolithic period and history reveals Roman, Anglo-Saxon and Norman settlements. Its importance grew in the Middle Ages, but it wasn't until the 18th century that Brighton's star really soared, when its handsome Georgian terraces were built and the Prince Regent became a regular visitor. The arrival of the railway in 1841 brought the town within reach of day trippers from London and many

Royal Pavilion

A bizarre seaside pleasure palace designed by Henry Holland and built (1787-1823) for the future George IV, the Royal Pavilion is based on Indo-Saracenic architecture prevalent in India at the time. Its exotic appearance – with its riot of domes and minarets – is the work of John Nash, who extended the building from 1815, and its interior is just as extravagant.

of its attractions were constructed during the Victorian era.

Among the town's must-see attractions is the amazing **Royal Pavilion** (see box, fee) and **Pavilion Gardens**, the adjoining **Brighton Museum & Art Gallery** (fee), which houses a wide-ranging collection of art and artefacts, and the **Brighton Dome**, built in 1803-6 as the Prince Regent's stables, and now the south coast's leading arts venue. Other attractions include the 1,722ft **Palace Pier**, which opened in 1899 and features a funfair, restaurants and arcade halls – one of the UK's finest piers, it attracts some five million visitors annually.

Palace Pier

Some 100m to the west, the ruins of the **West Pier** rise out of the sea. Built in 1866, it has been closed since 1975 and has suffered extensive damage from fires and storms rendering it beyond practical repair.

St Nicholas Church

Also worth seeking out is **St Nicholas Church**, dedicated to St Nicholas of Myra (patron saint of sailors, fishermen – and children), which can trace its origins back to the 14th century; **St Peter's Church** (1824-28), one of the UK's finest examples of pre-Victorian Gothic Revival architecture; **Brighton Clock Tower**, built in 1888 to commemorate Queen Victoria's Golden Jubilee; **Volk's Electric Railway** (opened 1883, fee) which runs along the seafront and is the world's oldest operating electric railway; and the 21st-century **British Airways i360** (2016, fee), an observation tower perched 531ft above the old West Pier entrance, affording panoramic views of the town and coastline.

The town's endless list of entertainments also includes the **Brighton Centre** for music, comedy and events; the **Theatre Royal**, founded in 1807; **Sea Life Brighton** (fee), built in 1872 and the world's oldest aquarium; and a host of museums. And then there's **Brighton Marina**, some beautiful parks and gardens and – not least – the town's 5½-mile shingle beach. If shopping is your thing, **The Lanes** is a must-visit, a series of narrow pedestrianised streets and alleys in the historic 16th-century centre, packed with a surfeit

Food & Drink

- **Redroaster Café:** Occupying a former post office on St James's Street, the Redroaster has an organic roastery and serves creative brunch and lunch dishes (7/8am-5pm, £).
- **Riddle & Finns:** Located in the Lanes, highly acclaimed R&F is a superb seafood restaurant (no reservations, 11.30am/noon-10/11pm, ££).

of independent shops, high street names, jewelers, antiques stores, cafés and bars. And when you're peckish, Brighton offers a world of gastronomic delights to suit every palate and pocket.

View from British Airways i360

Deal

i

Address: Deal, Kent CT14 7BB (aboutdeal.co.uk)

Rail: from 1h 22min via St Pancras International station

Road: 2h (88mi) via M2 and A2

Nearby: Dover, **Ramsgate**

A seaside resort and port in Kent, 88 miles from London, Deal is the quintessential English seaside town. A former fishing, mining and garrison town, Deal is mentioned in the *Domesday Book* (1086). In 1278 it joined the Cinque Ports – as a 'limb 'o' nearby Sandwich – and grew into the busiest port in England. Today, its quaint streets of higgledy-piggledy fishermen's cottages and Georgian townhouses – Middle Street was the first conservation area in Kent – are a reminder of its history, along with many ancient buildings and monuments.

Food & Drink

- **The Sir Normal Wisdom:** A popular Wetherspoon pub – named after the entertainer who lived in Deal as a child – offering real ales, craft beers and Lavazza coffee, and everything from breakfast to dinner (8am-midnight/1am, £).
- **81 Beach Street:** Smart seafront bistro serving modern British food with a European edge (01304-368136, noon-10pm, £-££).

Where better to start than **Deal Castle** (see box, fee), commissioned by Henry VIII as part of an ambitious chain of coastal forts, which included Walmer to the south and Sandown to the north. Recently refurbished, **Deal Pier** is the third in the town's history. The first – a wooden structure designed by Sir John Rennie and built in 1838 – was destroyed in a gale in 1864 and replaced by an iron pier that was severely damaged when it was struck by a mined ship in 1940. The current 1,026ft pier opened in 1957 and is the last remaining fully intact leisure pier in Kent, a popular fishing venue with a popular café-bar (Deal Pier Kitchen) at the end. A 10ft sculpture in front of its entrance, *Embracing the Sea* by Jon Buck (1998), pays homage to Deal's seafaring traditions.

Beach Street

Deal Castle

Built in 1539-40 on a Tudor rose floor plan, Deal Castle (English Heritage, fee) is an artillery fortress designed to allow all-round firepower from over 140 guns (although it only had

57 at its peak). One of the finest Tudor artillery castles in England, for over 250 years it defended the important naval anchorage of the Downs, and in 1648 was the stage for a hard-fought siege between Royalist and Parliamentarian forces during the English Civil War.

Other attractions include the town's lovely seafront promenade and pebble beach, with colourful fishing boats drawn up on the shingle. When you're hungry, Deal is home to a wide variety of restaurants, pubs and cafés, while the town's celebrated high street has intriguing shops, a produce market (Wed and Sat) in the **Town Hall** (1803), and a large Saturday market. If you're looking for some green space, **Betteshanger Park**, a 365-acre nature reserve on an old colliery site, is close by, along with the glorious **South Foreland Heritage Coast** – home to Dover's famous white cliffs – and the magnificent **Kent Downs** countryside.

You can discover more about the history of Deal at the **Deal Maritime & Local History Museum** (fee), which includes exhibits of boats, smugglers' galleys and model naval ships. Also part of Deal's maritime history is the **Deal Timeball Tower Museum** (fee) on the seafront, which tells the story of the

Timeball Tower

Victorian Greenwich Meantime Signal (GMT) located on its roof. Established in 1855, the time ball fell at 1pm precisely every day (triggered by an electric signal directly from the Royal Observatory in Greenwich) to relay the time to ships at sea.

Deal Pier

White Cliffs of Dover

Eastbourne

Address: Eastbourne, West Sussex BN21 3EL (visiteastbourne.com)

Rail: from 1h 33min via London Bridge station

Road: 2h 10min (83mi) via A267

Nearby: Brighton, Herstmonceux Castle, **Hastings**, Pevensey, Seaford

Located in East Sussex, 83 miles from London, Eastbourne is a fashionable seaside town developed in 1859 by William Cavendish (later the Duke of Devonshire) from four separate hamlets – a resort built 'for gentlemen by gentlemen'. Although a relatively new town, there's evidence of settlements in the area during the Stone Age and Roman, Anglo-Saxon and Norman periods. Evidence of Eastbourne's medieval past can be seen in the splendid 12th-century Church of St Mary the Virgin in the Old Town and Compton Place mansion house, while a number of historic buildings survive from the Georgian and Victorian periods.

Coastal Defences

Eastbourne Redoubt (open weekends, free) is a circular coastal defence fort built in 1805 at the same time as the Wish Tower and Martello Tower No 66 (overlooking Sovereign Harbour), two of 74 Martello Towers constructed along the south coast to defend against Napoleon in the early 1800s.

St Mary the Virgin was built in the late 12th century from Caen stone (from Normandy) and was considerably enlarged in the 14th century. Its massive greensand tower housed six bells in 1651, which was increased to eight in 1818. Nearby is **Gildredge Manor**, built by the Reverend Dr Henry Lushington (the vicar of Eastbourne) in 1776 on the site of a former inn, and next to it, beautiful **Manor Gardens** and **Gildredge Park**. **Compton Place** (Grade I listed) was originally a 16th-century Elizabethan/Jacobean manor house which was extensively remodelled in the early 18th century by Spencer Compton, 1st Earl of Wilmington, who renamed it Compton Place. It's now owned by the Duke of Devonshire.

Eastbourne's **Shingle Beach** stretches for around four miles from **Sovereign Harbour Marina** – Europe's largest composite marina – in the east to **Beachy Head** in the west. **Eastbourne Pier**, built 1866-1872, was destroyed during a

St Mary the Virgin

Eastbourne Beach

Grand Hotel

storm in 1877 and rebuilt. The replacement 1,000ft pier was placed on stilts, which rest in cups on the seabed and allow it to move during turbulent weather. Various traditional pier theatres have been built over the years, the last destroyed by fire in 1970 and replaced by the existing nightclub and bar. Today, it's one the finest examples of a Victorian pier in England with a café/bar, tea rooms, chippy, an amusement arcade, camera obscura and assorted shops and kiosks. A short distance from the pier is **Southbourne Bandstand**, which stages some 150 concerts a year.

For culture and history lovers, Eastbourne offers the renowned **Towner Art Gallery** (free) which displays a collection of over 4,500 works and is particularly noted for its modern British art; the **RNLI Lifeboat Museum** (free), housed in an old boathouse, dedicated to the local history of lifeboats since 1822; and the **Eastbourne Heritage Centre** (fee, local history). There are a number of theatres, too, including the **Winter Garden**. When you fancy stretching your

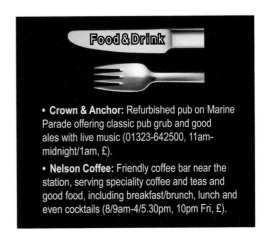

Food&Drink

• **Crown & Anchor:** Refurbished pub on Marine Parade offering classic pub grub and good ales with live music (01323-642500, 11am-midnight/1am, £).

• **Nelson Coffee:** Friendly coffee bar near the station, serving speciality coffee and teas and good food, including breakfast/brunch, lunch and even cocktails (8/9am-4/5.30pm, 10pm Fri, £).

legs, Eastbourne has some beautiful parks and gardens, while to the southwest is **Beachy Head** and the glorious **South Downs**. Food options range from fish 'n' chips to fine dining, while shoppers will delight in the streets of Victorian Little Chelsea and charming Meads Village.

Beachy Head

Eastbourne Pier

Hastings

> **Address:** Hastings, East Sussex TN34 1JY
> (visit1066country.com)
>
> **Rail:** from 1h 29min via St Pancras International
> and Charing Cross stations
>
> **Road:** 2h (76mi) via A21
>
> **Nearby:** Battle, Bexhill-on-Sea, Bodiam Castle,
> Dungeness, **Eastbourne**

Famous for the Battle of Hastings in 1066 – fought eight miles north of the town at Senlac Hill, where the remains of **Battle Abbey** (1094, fee) now stand – Hastings in East Sussex (76 miles from London) is a popular cosmopolitan seaside resort. At the time of the Norman Conquest Hastings was a thriving fishing village and is still home to the largest beach-launched fishing fleet in Europe. After the conquest, the town became one of the original five Cinque Ports, established by royal charter in 1155, which provided ships and men to

Hastings Castle

guard the country from attacks in return for certain privileges.

Hastings was the site of the first castle built in England by William the Conqueror. The original **Hastings Castle** was a motte-and-bailey castle constructed in 1066, which was rebuilt in stone in 1070. Over the centuries the castle saw many battles and today only ruins (open Mar-Oct, fee) remain, accessed from the Old Town via the **West Hill**

Food & Drink

- **The Crown:** An independent free house on All Saints Street, with delicious home-cooked food and craft beers on the menu and local art on the walls (01424-465100, 11am-11/10.30pm, £-££).

- **Maggie's:** Popular licensed fish restaurant on Fisherman's Beach offering fresh fish and seafood (01424-430205, lunch noon-3pm, closed Mon, £).

Panoramic view of Hastings

Hastings Pier

Originally built in 1872, the pier's 2,000-seat pavilion was destroyed by fire in 1917. Rebuilt in 1922, the pier enjoyed its heyday in the '30s and was a popular music venue in the '60s. Storm damage caused its closure in 1990 and it was destroyed by fire in 2010. However, a restored pier emerged from the ashes in 2016 and won the prestigious Stirling Prize for architecture the following year.

Lift. The **Old Town** is a delightful mixture of narrow streets and passageways, called 'twittens', handsome half-timbered houses, atmospheric pubs (e.g. **Ye Olde Pumphouse** in George Street) and shops. It's also home to the **Shipwreck Museum** and the **Fishermen's Museum** (both free), which recall the town's old seafaring days and famous local sunken ships. Next door stand the striking black **Net Huts** of Hastings Fish Market.

If you wish to learn more about the town's history, then **Hastings Museum & Art Gallery** (free) is a must; established for over 120 years, it contains a fascinating collection of more than 100,000 objects of local history, fine and decorative arts and natural sciences. If you're a fan of modern art, **Jerwood Gallery** (fee) on the seafront displays a superb collection of 20th- and 21st-century British art. Other attractions include the **Blue Reef Aquarium**, **Smugglers Adventure** in

St Clement's Caves, the **Miniature Railway**, the **White Rock Theatre** and the **Flamingo Park**. Like many of England's south coast beaches, Hastings beach is predominantly shingle, although there's a wide expanse of sand as the tide goes out.

The **East Hill Lift** (fee) is the UK's steepest funicular railway, providing access to **Hastings Country Park** at the top of East Hill – 660 acres of ancient woodland, grassland and heathland stretching across five miles of exposed cliffs and rugged terrain – while to the north of the town is lovely 109-acre **Alexandra Park**. There's plenty for shoppers in the Old Town, while the High Street has a range of independent boutiques and antiques shops. And when you're famished, Hastings offers an abundance of restaurants, cafés and pubs.

Net Huts

Fishing Boats

Leigh-on-Sea

Address: Leigh-on-Sea, Essex SS9 2EN
Rail: from 49min via Liverpool Street station
Road: 1h 5min (38mi) via A13
Nearby: Canvey Island, Southend-on-Sea

Said to be one of the happiest places to live in the UK, Leigh-on-Sea in Essex (just 38 miles from London) is a place of unique character and charm – a genteel town of narrow cobbled streets and timber-framed

houses – with miles of sandy beaches. The westernmost suburb of the borough of Southend-on-Sea on the north bank of the Thames estuary, Leigh is a former fishing village dating back some 1,000 years; the *Domesday Book* (1086) recorded 'five smallholders above the water who do not hold land', suggesting that fishing was an important trade even in the 11th century, with shellfish and whitebait the main catch.

Southend-on-Sea

While visiting Leigh it's worth taking the opportunity to see **Southend Pier**, the longest pier in the world at 7,080ft (1.34mi), with its own railway and lifeboat station. Originally built in 1830 and later extended, it was replaced by an iron pier in 1889. Southend is also home to the **Adventure Island** amusement park and the **Sea Life Adventure** aquarium, along with a number of museums, galleries and a planetarium.

Old Leigh (aka the Old Town) was an important settlement in the Middle Ages when it was on the main shipping route to London. In the 16th century it was a prosperous port, although by the mid-1700s its deep-water access had become silted up and the village went into decline. When the railway link from London to Southend was built in the mid-19th century, much of the old town was demolished to accommodate the railway's route, and new housing and streets began to be built on the hills above the settlement.

The parish church of **St Clement's** (Grade II* listed) was rebuilt in the late 15th century or early 16th century – much altered since – although records show a church here as far back as 1248. In the churchyard is a memorial to Leigh's fishermen who rescued British troops stranded on the beaches of Dunkirk in 1940. **Leigh Library** occupies the former rectory built in 1838 – although only a quarter of the original building remains – and there are a number of listed houses in the old town. You can learn about the town's history at the **Leigh Heritage Centre & Museum** (free), housed in the old smithy on the seafront. For lovers of historic buildings, neighbouring Southend is home to two stunning (Grade I listed) buildings: **Prittlewell Priory** (free), a 13th-century Cluniac monastery in Priory Park with beautiful ornamental walled gardens, and **Southchurch Hall** (free), a 14th-century Tudor moated manor house (not far from the pier).

Today, regenerated Leigh prides itself on its abundance of independent retailers, including many characterful boutiques, galleries, studios and craft shops. And when you're hungry, the town offers everything from fine dining to fast food, including some superb fish restaurants and cockle sheds. When you wish to stretch your legs you can stroll along the seafront to Southend (three miles) via Leigh Cliffs East, Chalkwell and Westcliff, while to the west are the beautiful nature reserves of **Belton Hills** and **Two Tree Island**.

Food & Drink

• **The Peterboat:** 17th-century inn with a huge terrace overlooking the estuary, famous for its excellent fish dishes and cockle shed (01702-475666, 10am-10.30/midnight, £).

• **Sara's Tea Garden:** Family-run café/tea shop with a charming garden offering cakes, cream teas and light lunches – plus a menu for dogs! (01702-477315, 10am-4/5pm, £).

Harbour Views

Margate

Address: Margate, Kent CT9 1XP (visitthanet.
co.uk/see-and-do/margate)

Rail: from 1h 27min via St Pancras International
and Victoria stations

Road: 1h 50min (82mi) via A2 and M2

Nearby: Broadstairs, **Ramsgate**

Lying on the northeast coast of Kent, 82 miles from London, Margate is a traditional English seaside town with an abundance of attractions and a lovely sandy beach. It's one of three classic Georgian/Victorian resorts on the Isle of Thanet – the other two are Broadstairs and Ramsgate (see page 98) – each with its own distinctive character. Until recently, Margate's image was that of a slightly down-at-heel, Cockney playground, but a regeneration scheme has helped it shed its kiss-me-quick persona and it's now one of the southeast's trendiest destinations.

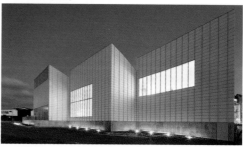

Turner Contemporary

Margate's **Old Town** rejoices in a cool vibe, where chic eateries, galleries and vintage shops exist alongside nostalgic (kitsch!) seaside delights. **Margate Museum** tells the history of the town as a sea-bathing and day-tripper destination, going back some 250 years, while nearby **Tudor House** has been home to master mariners, Flemish weavers, cordwainers and farmers since 1525. Other attractions include the internationally-

Food & Drink

- **Buoy & Oyster:** Award-winning, family-run restaurant and bar on Marine Drive with a terrace overlooking the beach, specialising in fish and seafood (01843-446631, lunch noon-3.30pm, seafood bar noon-9/10pm, ££).

- **Café G:** Rustic café in the old town with an outdoor terrace serving speciality coffee and light bites (9am-5.30pm, Sat/Sun 10am, £).

Main Sands

Dreamland

Margate has long been famous for its Dreamland amusement park. First opened in 1880, it became the great British seaside experience with historic rides – its rollercoaster dates from 1920 and is the second-oldest in the world – and classic side shows. The park's heyday was in the '60s and '70s and it went into a sharp decline in the early '00s, but was saved by a public campaign and is now making a comeback.

The town has two notable theatres, the **Theatre Royal** – a Georgian gem dating from 1787 and one of the oldest theatre in the country – and the **Tom Thumb**, the second-smallest in the UK. The celebrated **Winter Gardens** (1911) host a wide variety of concerts and events. Once a culinary desert, Margate is now a foodie hotspot, from fine dining to fast food and everything in between, while if you fancy a spot of shopping the town's cobbled streets are home to a cornucopia of independent shops, boutiques and galleries. If you want to stretch your legs, Margate has plenty of parks, while the more adventurous can take the **Viking Coastal Path** to nearby Botany Bay (2½ miles) or even Broadstairs (5½ miles).

acclaimed **Turner Contemporary** gallery (free) – named for J.M.W. Turner who liked to paint Margate's sunsets – which opened in 2011, showcasing historical and contemporary art works and sparking the town's regeneration. Margate is also home to the **Hornby Visitor Centre** (fee), beloved of model railway enthusiasts, and the amazing **Shell Grotto** (fee), an ornate subterranean passageway where the walls and roof (around 2,000ft^2) are covered in mosaics created with over 4½ million shells.

Margate is rightly famous for its wide sandy beach (Margate Main Sands) but is also noted for the **Walpole Bay Tidal Pool**, the UK's largest saltwater bathing pool, built in 1937 and extending to four acres. Margate Pier (1856) was destroyed in the great storm of January 1978, which caused extensive coastal flooding and widespread damage.

Kingsgate Bay

Main Sands

Mersea Island

Address: Mersea Island, Essex CO5 8NA
(visitmerseaisland.co.uk)

Rail: from 46min to Colchester via Liverpool
Street, then taxi/bus to Mersea Island (9mi)

Road: 1h 40min (69mi) via A12

Nearby: Clacton-on-Sea, **Colchester**

Note

Before setting off ensure you check the tide times
(tidetimes.org.uk/west-mersea-tide-times) as the
main access to the island is via an artificial causeway
known as The Strood, which is often covered at high
tide, especially during spring tides.

Mersea Island (7mi²) in Essex, 69 miles from London,
is the UK's most easterly inhabited island, located
in the estuary of the Blackwater and Colne rivers,
nine miles southeast of Colchester. It's divided into
two main areas, West Mersea, the main residential

The Rev Sabine Baring-Gould, rector of the Church
of St Edmund from 1871-1881, was a prolific writer
and scholar, and the author of one of England's most
famous hymns, *Onward Christian Soldiers*.

area containing the jetty and marina, and East Mersea
which is predominantly farmland. The island has been
inhabited since pre-Roman times and is believed to have
been a 'holiday' destination for the Roman garrison at
Colchester. Fishing and oyster farming have been key
industries on the island (supplemented by smuggling!)
since the 16th and 17th centuries when Dutch and
French settlers arrived and, along with tourism, they still
make up the bulk of the island's economy.

The old town
of West Mersea
is home to
a number of
listed buildings,
including the
parish **Church
of St Peter
& St Paul**,
thought to
have been

St Peter & St Paul

founded in the 7th century and rebuilt after
destruction by Norse raiders in 894. The west
tower was added to the church around the 11th
century, the south aisle in the 15th century, plus
various other rebuilds up to the end of the 18th
century. The **Church of St Edmund** in East
Mersea dates from the 12th-13th centuries.

Beach Huts, West Mersea

Food & Drink

- **The Artcafé:** Good place for breakfast/brunch, coffee or lunch, with paintings by local artists for sale (9am-5pm, £).
- **The Company Shed:** Arrive early for lunch at this renowned seafood restaurant with a BYO booze/bread policy (01206-382700, 9am-4pm, Sun 10am, closed Mon, £-££). A good alternative is the West Mersea Oyster Bar (01206-381600, 9am-4/5pm, Fri-Sat 10pm, £).

The island's laid-back atmosphere, cute weatherboard cottages, ramshackle houseboats, colourful beach huts, sandy beaches, beautiful sea and country views and fine seafood restaurants, make for a relaxing day trip far from the madding crowds.

Company Shed

The rich history of Mersea Island can be explored at the local **Mersea Museum** (fee), close to St Peter & St Paul.

Not surprisingly, Mersea Island is all about the great outdoors, with its unspoilt beaches, stunning countryside, expansive estuary views and lovely walks. Most of the area immediately surrounding the island consists of saltmarsh and mudflats, an important sanctuary for wading and migratory birds. In East Mersea is **Cudmore Grove Country Park** (102 acres) with a sandy beach, rolling grasslands and meadows buzzing with wildlife. Beachcombers may find fossils here – shark's teeth and even hippo bones have been unearthed. In summer there are boat trips around the estuary on the *Lady Grace*, while in winter you can hire a boat for a fishing expedition or view the wading birds feeding on the mudflats.

Lady Grace

Ramsgate

Address: Ramsgate, Kent CT11 9FT
(ramsgatetown.org)

Rail: from 1h 39min via St Pancras and other
stations

Road: 1h 55min (84mi) via M2

Nearby: Broadstairs, Deal, Margate

Food & Drink

• **The Galley:** Popular café overlooking the
harbour, great for breakfast, lunch, afternoon tea
and stunning views (8am-6pm, £).

• **Royal Victoria Pavilion:** Vast JD Wetherspoon
pub occupying the striking former Pavilion (with
opulent loos), serving JD's usual pub grub plus
authentic pizzas (8am-midnight/1am, £).

One of England's great seaside resorts of the 19th
century, Ramsgate on the Isle of Thanet in Kent (84
miles from London) has one of the largest marinas on
the south coast and glorious golden sands. The town
began as a hamlet dependent on fishing and farming,
visited (or invaded) by Vikings, Anglo-Saxons, Romans
and St Augustine, who landed here in AD597. Ramsgate
was also an associate member of the confederation of
Cinque Ports as a 'limb' of Sandwich.

The town is noted for its elegant
Georgian terraces and impressive
Regency villas – it boasts some 900
listed buildings – alongside some fine
Victorian buildings. The latter include
the home of architect Augustus Pugin
(1812-52), who designed the interiors
of the Houses of Parliament. Pugin's
home, **The Grange** (guided tours,
fee), which he built in 1843, is next to
gorgeous **St Augustine's Church** and
shrine, designed by Pugin in 1847 and
his final resting place. Pugin also built

St Augustine's Abbey, across the road from the church.
The oldest building in Ramsgate is pretty **St Laurence's
Church** (Grade I listed), aka St Laurence-in-Thanet,
founded in 1062 and rebuilt after a lightning strike in
1439.

Ramsgate Harbour is England's only royal
harbour – as decreed by George IV in 1821 – and

Ramsgate Harbour

St Laurence's Church

When you've enjoyed lunch at one of the town's excellent harbour-side restaurants, cafés or pubs, hop on a boat trip to spot seals basking on the Goodwin Sands and discover beautiful beaches and bays. The port is at the centre of a network of clifftop walking trails, northeast to Broadstairs or south on the epic Saxon Shore Way to the Sandwich and Pegwell Bay Nature Reserve. If you fancy a spot of retail therapy before leaving, the old town is peppered with delightful shops and boutiques, while a few minutes away is **Petticoat Lane Emporium** on Dumpton Park Drive, with more than 175 stalls of antiques, crafts and curios.

boasts its own Meridian Line, five minutes and 41 seconds ahead of GMT, which you'll find in the **Maritime Museum** (fee). Housed in the Clock House on the quayside, the museum tells the story of the town's rich seafaring heritage of fishing, lifeboats, shipbuilding and shipwrecks. The sheltered harbour was built between 1749 and 1850 as a response to the great storm of 1703, which saw the loss of much shipping and was the worst disaster to befall the Royal Navy in peacetime. During the Second World War, Ramsgate's residents sheltered from the bombing in the famous **Ramsgate Tunnels** (fee), almost four miles long with a capacity of 60,000.

Vincent Van Gogh

Ramsgate was briefly home to the artist Vincent Van Gogh, who moved to the town in 1876 at the age of 23. He boarded at 11 Spencer Square – identified by a blue plaque – and worked as a teacher at a local school.

Main Sands

Royal Viking Pavilion

Whitstable

Address: Whitstable, Kent CT5 1AB
(seewhitstable.com)

Rail: from 1h 14min via St Pancras and Victoria
stations

Road: 1h 30min (66mi) via M2

Nearby: Canterbury, Chilham, Faversham, Isle
of Sheppey

A seaside resort and fishing 'village' on the north coast of Kent, 66 miles from London, Whitstable is famous for its oysters – celebrated in the summer Whitstable Oyster Festival – but offers much more. Archaeological finds indicate that the area was inhabited during the Palaeolithic, Bronze and Iron Age periods. The town's development as a seaside resort began in the late 18th century and its attractive shingle beaches include popular Tankerton Beach east of the harbour. At low tide a half-mile strip of shingle called The Street allows you to walk out to sea for a gull's eye view of the beach, with its wooden groynes (barriers) and multi-coloured beach huts (watch out for the tide!).

Whitstable grew from a village on the main road to Canterbury, and its numerous meandering alleyways developed as local residents needed better access to the sea (they also served as escape routes for smugglers!). **Island Wall**, the closest street to the seafront, has numerous 19th-century buildings, including Dollar Row cottages, built from the proceeds of salvaging a ship carrying silver dollars.

The town's most famous landmark is **Whitstable Castle**, which started life as Tankerton Towers in the late 1790s. It's now an events venue and is closed to the general public, but the castle's magnificent gardens (and Orangery Tearooms) are well worth a look, and it's just a few minutes' walk from the harbour. **St Alphege Church** on the High Street was built in the 1840s to replace a small medieval church at Seasalter. The **Horsebridge Arts**

Whitstable Harbour

Old Neptune pub

Centre has a striking 'upturned boat' design and contains an art gallery, performance space and art workshops.

If you're browsing for a bargain, head for charming Harbour Street and the High Street, with their pretty pastel-painted shops, boutiques and art galleries, and while there check out JD Wetherspoon's **Peter Cushing** pub, which occupies a striking Art Deco cinema and is named after the Hammer Horror star and former resident. Opposite the harbour is **Harbour Market**, an open-air showcase of hand-crafted goods and fine art, where local artists sell their paintings, drawings, prints and photography, alongside artisans making jewellery, wrought ironwork, ceramics, textiles and furniture.

Although Whitstable is famous for its seafood – oysters, crab, lobster, scallops, etc. – and fish, it isn't compulsory, and the town offers a wide variety of cuisines to suit every taste. When you want to walk off your lunch there are miles of beaches. If you're feeling energetic you can walk east to Herne Bay (five miles,

return by train) along the Saxon Shore Way – or take a stroll through Duncan Down just south of the town centre, 52 acres of woodland, scrubland, grassland and streams, providing a variety of wildlife habitats. Whitstable locals claim it's the largest 'village green' in England.

Whitstable Castle

Worthing

Address: Worthing, West Sussex BN11 3PX
(discoverworthing.uk)

Rail: from 1h 27min via London Bridge station

Road: 2h (62mi) via A24

Nearby: Arundel, Bognor Regis, **Brighton**,
Chichester

Food & Drink

• **The Egremont:** Elegant bar – specialising in
gin – and restaurant, offering tasty home-cooked
food, including vegan options (01903-600064,
noon-11pm, £-££).

• **Munch Coffee Bar & Kitchen:** Popular family-
owned café serving good coffee, delicious cakes
and savoury dishes (9.30am-4pm, £).

Worthing is a large seaside town in West Sussex, 62 miles from London, at the foot of the South Downs. The area has been inhabited for at least 6,000 years and contains Britain's greatest concentration of Stone Age flint mines, dating from around 4000BC. For many centuries Worthing was a small agricultural and fishing village, but in the 18th century it began to attract wealthy and influential visitors and developed into a Georgian/Regency seaside resort. Today, Worthing is an attractive blend of seaside tradition and genteel elegance.

The town's most important landmark is **Worthing Pier**, which was declared the best in Britain in 2019 by the National Piers Society. The first pier, designed by Sir Robert Rawlinson, opened in 1862; a simple promenade deck 960ft in length, it was upgraded in 1888 when a 650-seat pavilion was built. In 1933 the pier was destroyed by fire and was replaced in 1935 by the Streamline Moderne Art Deco design that you see today. In 1940 the pier was partly dismantled and a large hole was blown in it to prevent the enemy using it as a landing stage in the event of a German invasion.

If old buildings are your thing, the suburb of **West Tarring** is worth a visit. Here you'll find St Andrew's Church and the Archbishop's Palace – both dating from the 13th century – and numerous

Worthing Pier

Worthing Lido

In the late 19th century Oscar Wilde was a visitor – he wrote *The Importance of Being Earnest* in Worthing – while playwright Harold Pinter lived at 14 Ambrose Place in the '60s, marked by a blue plaque.

historic houses, including 15th-century, timber-framed Parsonage Row. Worthing town centre features some worthy buildings from the late Georgian and Regency periods, including **St Paul's Church**. Opened in 1812 as the Worthing Chapel of Ease, it has a striking Doric portico with four columns. The elegant **Beach House** on Brighton Road was built in 1820, and gives its name to nearby Beach House Park, a famous lawn bowls venue, while **Colonnade House** is one of the town's most iconic architectural landmarks – built in the early 1800s and re-modelled in Art Deco style after a fire in the '30s. It's now home to a gallery showcasing work by painters, printmakers, sculptors and photographers.

The superb **Worthing Museum & Art Gallery** (free) is housed in a 1908 building, originally designed as the town's library (funded by Andrew Carnegie) along with the museum. It contains one of the UK's largest costume and textile collections, an important collection of Georgian dolls and toys, plus collections relating to social history, numismatics, and fine and decorative art.

When it comes to entertainment Worthing has a number of excellent venues, including the **Connaught Theatre** built in 1914, the **Pavilion Theatre** at the end of the pier, the **Worthing Lido** and the **Dome Cinema**, one of Britain's oldest picture houses opened

in 1911. There's a wealth of restaurants, cafés and bars to suit every taste. And if you need to walk off any over-indulgence there are lovely promenade walks and the nearby **South Downs National Park**. If you want to splash the cash, Worthing offers the elegant **Royal Arcade Shopping Mall** along with many independent shops.

Beach House

Royal Arcade

Beach

Leeds Castle, Kent (see page 118)

4.
Stately Homes

England has a wealth of stately homes, many within under 90 minutes (or less) by train from London. They include the World Heritage site of Blenheim Palace in Oxfordshire; Winston Churchill's family home, Chartwell, in Kent; Hatfield House (Herts.), former home of Queen Elizabeth I; Highclere Castle in Berkshire, aka Downton Abbey; picturesque Leeds Castle in Kent (the 'castle of queens'); and Neo-Renaissance Waddesdon Manor in Buckinghamshire, built by Baron Ferdinand de Rothschild.

Note that stately homes often have restricted opening times, particularly in winter, when some are closed altogether. Prices can be very high, especially for families; sometimes there are separate prices for visiting a park/garden and the stately home itself. If you're planning to visit a number of stately homes or other grand buildings (or parks and gardens - see **Chapter 5**) owned or managed by the National Trust and/or English Heritage, it may be worthwhile joining the relevant organisation. However, bear in mind that a couple need to visit at least three properties a year to recoup the cost of membership.

Blenheim Palace

Address: Blenheim Palace, Woodstock, Oxfordshire OX20 1UL (blenheimpalace.com)

Rail: from 1h 6min to Hanborough via Paddington station, then 233 bus/taxi (3mi)

Road: 1h 30min (65mi) via M40

Opening Hours: park 9am-6pm, palace 10.30am-5.30pm

Fees: palace, park & gardens £27 (child £16), park & gardens £17 (child £7.60)

Nearby: Bicester, **Cotswolds**, **Oxford**, **Waddesdon**

The palace was the birthplace of Sir Winston Churchill (1874-1965) and served as a convalescence hospital during the First World War, while during the Second World War over 400 boys were evacuated to the palace from Malvern College.

One of the most popular tourist attractions in the UK, monumental Blenheim Palace near Woodstock, Oxfordshire (65 miles from London), is one of Britain's most important stately homes – with 187 rooms – and has been a World Heritage Site since 1987. It was built between 1705 and 1722 to celebrate the victory over the French in the War of the Spanish Succession (1701–14), a conflict between European powers over who had the right to succeed Charles II of Spain, the last of the Spanish Habsburgs. The palace was a gift from Queen Anne to John Churchill, 1st Duke of Marlborough (1650-1722), who led the allied forces in the Battle of Blenheim on 13th August 1704. In the north of the park stands a 134ft *Column of Victory* crowned by a statue of the duke dressed as a Roman general.

Saloon

The palace – the only non-royal, non-episcopal country house in England to hold the title of palace – was designed by Sir

Blenheim Palace

John Vanbrugh and Nicholas Hawksmoor, and is a rare example of 18th-century English Baroque architecture, an exuberant style that originated in late 16th-century Italy. The palace has been the home of the Churchill (later Spencer-Churchill) family for the last 300 years. At the end of the 19th century Blenheim was saved from ruin by funds gained through the 9th Duke of Marlborough's calculated marriage to American railroad heiress Consuelo Vanderbilt in 1895.

Visitors can tour the splendid state rooms, which contain one of the most important and extensive collections in Europe, including portraits, furniture, sculpture and tapestries. The (Winston) Churchill Exhibition is a permanent presentation of the great man's life, while the Untold Story is an interactive experience revealing the personal history of the palace's inhabitants. There are also 'Upstairs' and 'Downstairs' tours for an additional fee, revealing how guests – and servants – lived.

Blenheim sits in the centre of a large undulating park (2,000-plus acres) with 90 acres of formal gardens – by Henry Wise, Queen Anne's gardener – designed in the formal style of Versailles. The landscaped parkland was created over ten years from 1764 by landscape architect Lancelot 'Capability' Brown, who constructed the Great Lake and planted thousands of trees to fashion a classic example of the English landscape garden movement.

Today, Blenheim Palace is unique in its combined use as a family home, mausoleum and national monument. The palace chapel, designed by William Kent, is the last resting place of the 1st Duke of Marlborough, while the palace remains the home of the Dukes of Marlborough – the present incumbent is Charles James (Jamie) Spencer-Churchill, the 12th Duke.

Food & Drink

- **Orangery Restaurant:** Enjoy lunch or afternoon tea in the stunning setting of the glass-roofed orangery (book via website, lunch noon-2pm, ££).
- **Water Terrace Café:** Caféteria-style restaurant overlooking the beautiful water terraces, serving sandwiches, seasonal hot meals and a wide range of drinks (10am-5.30pm, £).

Blenheim stages a variety of cultural events throughout the year and is also home to the Pleasure Gardens which feature giant games, an adventure playground, maze and butterfly house, and is linked to the palace by a miniature train. There are a number of on-site cafés and a restaurant (see **Food & Drink** box) serving everything from champagne to pizza.

Palace Gardens

Chartwell

Address: Chartwell, Mapleton Road, Westerham, Kent TN16 1PS (nationaltrust.org.uk/chartwell)

Rail: from 40min to Oxted via Victoria station, then 236 bus/taxi (5mi)

Road: 1h 15min (26mi) via A215 or M25 (junc 6)

Opening Hours: garden 10am-5pm, house 11.30am-5pm (see website, as times vary depending on the season)

Fees: timed tickets, £15.50 (child £7.75), garden/studio only £9 (child £4.50), parking £4

Nearby: Emmetts Garden, Sevenoaks, Royal Tunbridge Wells

The much-loved family home and garden of Sir Winston Churchill (1874-1965) for over 40 years, Chartwell (Grade I listed) near Westerham, Kent (26 miles from London), is a monument to one of England's greatest leaders. The origins of the estate can be traced back to 1382 when the property was sold by William-At-Well. It passed through various owners until, in 1848, it was purchased by John Campbell Colquhoun, whose grandson sold it to Churchill in 1922. Between 1922 and 1924 it was largely rebuilt by architect Philip Tilden.

Churchill was a prolific painter and his studio is home to the largest collection of his paintings, where his paints are laid out with a canvas awaiting completion, as if the great man had just popped out for a cigar and a glass of champagne.

In the '30s, when Churchill was out of public office, Chartwell became the centre of his world. At his dining table he gathered friends and allies who supported his campaign against German re-armament; in his study he composed speeches and wrote books; while in the garden he built walls, constructed lakes and painted. During the Second World War Chartwell was largely unused, although the Churchills returned in 1945 after Winston lost the general election. In October 1964 Churchill left Chartwell for the last time, dying at his London home on 24th January 1965. After his death the house became the property of the National Trust (who had purchased it in 1945) and it was opened to the public in 1966.

Chartwell

Food & Drink

- **Grasshopper On The Green:** Believed to be around 700 years old, the Grasshopper in Westerham is a cosy spot for a home-cooked lunch and a pint of local ale (01959-562926, 10am-10.30pm/midnight, £).
- **Landemare Café:** In-house café with an outdoor terrace, offering coffee/tea, cakes, lunch and cream teas (10am-5pm, £).

From its garden, Chartwell enjoys extensive views over the Weald of Kent, "the most beautiful and charming" that Churchill had ever seen and the determining factor in his decision to buy the house. The hillside gardens (20 acres) and parkland (57 acres) reflect his love of the landscape and nature, and include the lakes he created (complete with black swans), kitchen garden, rose walk and the Marycot, a playhouse designed for his youngest daughter Mary. Beyond the gardens there's an expanse of woodland with looped trails, natural play areas and plenty of opportunities to stretch your legs.

There's the usual excellent on-site NT café and you can picnic in the meadow (off the car park) or by the lake on the lower lawn.

Drawing Room

Today, the rooms remain much as they were when Churchill lived there – decorated as they were in the '30s – with pictures, books and personal mementoes evoking the career and wide-ranging interests of the statesman, writer, painter and family man. As you make your way around the house, the rooms – library, study, sitting and dining rooms – are presented as if the family had just stepped out, and there are plans to open Churchill's bedroom in the near future. The many fascinating objects on display include gifts that Churchill received, uniforms and items from the family collection.

Sir Winston Churchill

Churchill's Study

Hatfield House

Address: Hatfield House, Great North Road, Hatfield, Herts AL9 5HX (hatfield-house.co.uk)

Rail: from 27min via King's Cross station

Road: 1h 5min (23mi) via A1 (M)

Opening Hours: house Wed-Sun 11am-5pm, garden Tue-Sun 10.30am-5pm

Fees: house and garden £19 (child £9), garden only £11 (child £7)

Nearby: Brocket Hall, Hertford, **Knebworth House, St Albans**

Food & Drink

- **River Cottage Kitchen & Deli:** From a snack to a three-course meal, the on-site River Cottage works in partnership with food campaigner Hugh Fearnley-Whittingstall, so you're sure of tasty seasonal food (10am-5pm, closed Mon, £).
- **Stable Yard Coffee Shop:** At the bottom of the yard, this cosy coffee shop offers a variety of coffees, cakes and pastries (10am-5pm, £).

Home of the 7th Marquess and Marchioness of Salisbury, Hatfield House in Hertfordshire (23 miles from London) is one of the largest and most impressive Jacobean mansions in England. It was built in 1611 by Robert Lyminge for Robert Cecil, 1st Earl of Salisbury, Chief Secretary and Lord High Treasurer to James I. Cecil didn't live to enjoy the house and died (aged just 48) in April 1612; he's buried at Hatfield, which has been the home of his descendants for 400 years. The estate includes extensive grounds and surviving parts of an earlier palace (see box), which was closely associated with Elizabeth I.

Superb examples of Jacobean craftsmanship can be seen throughout the house, which was splendidly decorated for entertaining the royal court, with state rooms rich in paintings, fine furniture and tapestries. The carved wooden Grand Staircase – with its snarling lions and winsome cherubs – and the rare stained-glass window in the private chapel are among the original Jacobean features. If the house looks familiar it's starred in umpteen films and TV series, from *Lara Croft: Tomb Raider* to *The Favourite* (where it was Queen Anne's home).

Many historic mementoes collected over the centuries by the Cecil family are on display, as are a number of objects associated with

Hatfield House

Elizabeth I, including a pair of silk stockings that are believed to have been the first in England. The library contains a 22-foot illuminated parchment roll showing the pedigree of the Queen (with ancestors going back to Adam and Eve!), while the Marble Hall displays the famous *Rainbow Portrait* of Elizabeth (ca 1600) by Marcus Gheeraerts the Younger.

Long Gallery

An earlier building on the site was the Royal Palace of Hatfield, part of which still exists. Built in 1497 by the Bishop of Ely, Henry VII's minister John Cardinal Morton, it comprised four wings in a square around a central courtyard. Seized by Henry VIII along with other church properties, the Old Palace (as it's known) was the childhood home and favourite residence of Elizabeth I, who learned of her accession to the throne there in 1558.

The extensive gardens of Hatfield House (42 acres) date from the early 17th century and were laid out by John Tradescant the Elder, including orchards, fountains, scented plants, water parterres, terraces, herb gardens and a maze. A modern addition is the imposing water sculpture, *Renaissance*, by Angela Conner (2015), which takes pride of place on the North Front of Hatfield House.

Queen Elizabeth I

Today, the West Garden is home to a scented garden, fountains and a fascinating Longitude dial, while the East Garden (open on Weds) is more formal, with a parterre, topiary, herbaceous borders and vegetable garden. There's also a famous knot garden adjoining the Old Palace. The spectacular gardens and extensive parkland – which has a number of marked walks – encompass Hatfield Park Farm, complete with animals, a miniature train, play areas and a restaurant.

Gardens

Highclere Castle

it. Major rebuilding works in the late 18th and early 19th centuries saw the old red brick house converted into a classical Georgian country seat. However, its current incarnation was created in the mid-1800s when the 3rd Earl of Carnarvon appointed Sir Charles Barry to transform Highclere into a grand mansion, designed in Jacobethan style and faced in Bath stone.

Egyptian Exhibition

This exhibition in the castle's cellars tells the story of the discovery of the tomb of Tutankhamun. It's the legacy of the 5th Earl, who was an enthusiastic amateur Egyptologist and who sponsored and accompanied archaeologist Howard Carter during the discovery of the tomb in 1922.

Famous as the location for the British TV series *Downton Abbey*, the previously obscure Highclere Castle in Berkshire (66 miles from London) is now one of England's best-known stately homes. The castle stands on the site of an earlier house that was built on the foundations of the palace of the Bishops of Winchester. Later records reveal a medieval palace built during the 12th-13th centuries, which was succeeded by a much-admired red-brick Tudor house.

Highclere has been home to the Earls of Carnarvon since 1679, who have been instrumental in rebuilding and reinventing

The castle's splendid state rooms – saloon, drawing room, dining room, music room, library and smoking room – and even the bedrooms – are a familiar sight to *Downton Abbey* fans worldwide. The period drama's

Highclere Castle

Food&Drink

- **The Yew Tree:** Located close to Highclere, the Yew Tree Inn is a delightful 17th-century country pub offering superb British cuisine, plus rooms if you wish to stay over (01635-253360, lunch noon-2.30pm, 4pm Sun, £-££).
- **Tea Rooms:** On-site tea rooms serving cream teas, light lunches and hot meals (9.30am-4pm, £). You can also book a special 'Afternoon Tea at the Coach House' ticket.

and the filming of *Downton Abbey* (see website for information).

Set in 1,000 acres of sweeping parkland, Highclere was originally a deer park, gifted to the church of Winchester in 749. It has been tamed and planted over the centuries, and was transformed into a landscaped park for the 1st Earl of Carnarvon by Lancelot 'Capability' Brown in 1774-77. Highlights include some imaginative follies and 250-year-old cedar trees. Closer to the castle are the more formal gardens, including the Monks' Garden – recalling the former ecclesiastical keepers – where climbing roses put on a fine show in June; the gorgeous White Border with its pale splendour of roses, clematis, peonies and hydrangeas; and, through a gate, the captivating Secret Garden, where it's easy to imagine Lady Mary dallying with one of her suitors.

runaway success has boosted visitor numbers hugely and ticket sales have helped to fund much-needed repairs. The (real life) 8th Earl and Countess of Carnarvon now decamp to a nearby cottage during the summer months when the castle, its gardens and the Egyptian Exhibition (see box) are open to the public. As well as exploring the state rooms, bedrooms and servants' quarters, visitors can take a special tour (organised for small groups) themed around food, gardens

Dining Room

Library

Saloon

Knebworth House

Address: Knebworth House, Stevenage, Herts SG1 2AX (knebworthhouse.com)

Rail: from 43min to Stevenage via King's Cross station, then walk/taxi (1½mi)

Road: 1h 20min (32mi) via A1 (M)

Opening Hours: park/gardens 11am-5pm, house noon-5pm (closed Oct-Feb, see website for dates)

Fees: house & gardens £14 (child £13.50), gardens only £10 (child £10)

Nearby: Hatfield House, Hertford, Stevenage, St Albans

In 1913-1914 the house was leased by the exiled Grand Duke Michael Alexandrovich of Russia. He returned to Russia in 1914 and assumed command of a cavalry regiment, and when Tsar Nicholas abdicated in 1917, the Grand Duke was named as his successor. But he was never confirmed as Emperor and after the Russian Revolution in 1917 he was imprisoned and murdered by the Bolsheviks.

The home of the Lytton family since 1490, Knebworth House (Grade II* listed) is a striking manor house in Knebworth, Hertfordshire (just 32 miles from London), set in 250 acres of rolling countryside. Built by Sir Robert Lytton, who became Under Treasurer to Henry VII after the Battle of Bosworth, the original red-brick Tudor house is clad in Victorian High Gothic fantasy style, complete with turrets, spires, towers, domes, gargoyles and gryphons. The 19th-century remodelling was the work of its most famous resident, novelist and statesman Sir Edward Bulwer Lytton (1803-1873), who penned the immortal lines "it was a dark and stormy night" and "the pen is mightier than the sword".

Each generation of the Lytton family has added something of its style and taste to Knebworth, resulting in an extraordinary journey through 500 years of British history. Notable family members include Lady Emily Bulwer-Lytton (1874-1964), wife of Sir Edwin Lutyens, and Lady Constance Bulwer-Lytton (1869-1923) who was an influential Suffragette. Stories and heirlooms reflect the family's contribution to literature, politics and foreign service, and reveal the diverse range of characters to visit Knebworth, from Charles Dickens to Noel and Liam Gallagher.

Knebworth's interiors were styled by J G Grace and, later, by Sir Edwin Lutyens (1869-1944), while the panelled banqueting hall is by John Webb, the best-known pupil of Inigo Jones. A Jacobean minstrels' gallery hovers above the hall, where Charles Dickens liked to

Knebworth House

hold amateur theatricals when he visited. House tours include the British Raj Exhibition – which tells the story of the Lytton family's connection with India – and a costume display that brings the Elizabethan heritage of Knebworth House to life, with exquisite Tudor gowns, children's outfits, and a gentleman's doublet and hose.

The estate contains 28 acres of formal landscaped gardens, which include a sunken lawn with pollarded limes, walled gardens, Victorian statuary, sprawling shrub roses, a maze, mature trees and a wilderness area, along with a historic deer park. Also within the park – the perfect setting for picnics and walks – is 12th-century St Mary's Church (Grade I listed) and the Lytton family mausoleum, along with Fort Knebworth Adventure Playground and a Dinosaur Trail.

Knebworth hosts regular rallies and fairs, and has been an important rock festival venue since 1974, when the Allman Brothers Band entertained 60,000 fans. Some 20 years later in 1996, Oasis famously headlined, playing to more than 250,000 people over two nights – one of the biggest rock events in British history.

Food & Drink

- **Garden Terrace Tea Room:** Licensed, self-service tea room located in the on-site 16th-century tithe barn, offering cakes, soup, salads, sandwiches, ice cream and more (11am-5pm, £).
- **Lytton Arms:** Close to Knebworth House in Old Knebworth, this iconic real ale pub offers a wholesome rustic menu (01438-812312, 11am-11pm/midnight, £).

Bedroom

State Drawing Room

Library

Knole House

Address: Knole House, Sevenoaks, Kent TN13 1HX (nationaltrust.org.uk/knole)

Rail: from 32min to Sevenoaks via Charing Cross, then taxi/walk (1.6mi)

Road: 1h 10min (40mi) via A13 & M25

Opening Hours: park dawn to dusk, house 11am-5pm

Fees: whole property £15 (child £7.50), gatehouse £5 (child £2.50)

Nearby: Ightham Mote, Sevenoaks, Tonbridge

Food & Drink

- **Brewhouse Café:** Café in the former 17th-century brewhouse with a rooftop terrace, offering drinks, snacks, ice cream, hot meals and cream teas (10am-5pm, £).
- **White Hart:** 17th-century coaching inn located on the Tonbridge Road, the White Hart serves classic British fare (01732-452022, 11.30/noon-10.30/11pm, £-££).

Situated within Kent's last medieval deer park close to Sevenoaks (40 miles from London) overlooking the weald of Kent, Knole House offers something for everyone. The huge house – part owned and managed by the National Trust – ranks in the top five of England's largest houses, extending to almost 17,500ft^2 (4 acres) and said to have a room for each day of the year. The earliest recorded owner, in the 1290s, was Robert de Knole, although the current Grade I listed house dates from the mid-15th century, with major additions in the 16th and early 17th centuries. Originally built as an archbishop's palace, Knole passed through churchmen and royalty to the Sackville family, who still live there today. Poet, novelist, and garden designer Vita Sackville-West (1892-1962) grew up here (see **Sissinghurst Castle Garden** on page 144).

Beyond the Jacobean façade there's plentiful evidence of the earlier house, such as the northern range of Stone Court, an inner courtyard that leads to the state rooms. Many rooms are open to the public, showcasing the magnificent objects – paintings by Reynolds, Gainsborough and Van Dyck, 17th-century tapestries and Stuart furniture – that make the Sackvilles' collection internationally significant. (It's said that Charles Sackville, 6th Earl of Dorset, made the most of his position as

Knole House

Chamberlain of the Household to William and Mary to recycle the monarchs' cast-offs – and many of their furnishings found their way to Knole House.)

The decorative Great Staircase leads to a series of high-status apartments, such as the King's Bedroom with its solid silver furniture, prepared for a visit by James I, and the Spangle Bedroom which once contained a sequinned bed. The Gatehouse Tower, built in the 1540s, reveals the life and loves of a more recent resident, Eddy Sackville-West – Vita's cousin and a contemporary of the Bloomsbury Set – who lived in the tower between 1926 and 1940. Climb the spiral staircase to enjoy the panoramic views from the rooftop.

The scale and magnificence of the 600-year-old estate is best appreciated by exploring the grand courtyards or wandering the winding paths in the parkland. The garden at Knole dates back to the early 15th century and the walled garden – one of its oldest features – probably marked its original boundary at the time of Thomas Bourchier, Archbishop of Canterbury.

The area beyond the walled garden is known as 'the wilderness' and is much less formal than other parts of the garden, with mossy paths meandering through the trees to grassy clearings. The 1,000-acre Knole Park – home to a 350-strong deer herd – is popular with walkers, cyclists, and nature lovers.

Lord Sackville's private garden is a magical space, featuring sprawling lawns, a vast walled garden (26 acres) and a medieval orchard. It can be viewed on Tuesdays (Apr-Sep) via the beautiful Orangery, where the doors open to reveal the secluded lawns and majestic walkways of the Sackville family's private space.

Staircase

Knole Park

Ballroom

Leeds Castle

Address: Leeds Castle, Maidstone, Kent ME17 1RG (leeds-castle.com)

Rail: from around 1h to Bearsted via Victoria station, then shuttle bus (Apr-Sep)

Road: 1h 30min (43mi) via A2

Opening Hours: castle 10am-4/5.30pm, grounds and gardens 10am-5/6pm

Fees: £26 (child £17.50)

Nearby: Chatham, Maidstone, **Rochester, Sissinghurst Castle Garden**

Situated near the village of Leeds in Kent (not Yorkshire!), five miles east of Maidstone and 43 miles from London, Grade I listed Leeds Castle enjoys a spectacular setting in a lake formed by the River Len, its towers reflected in the water from almost every angle. Originally the site of a wooden structure built in 857 and owned by a Saxon chieftain called Led (or Leed), a castle has existed here since 1119. The first incarnation was a simple stone stronghold constructed by Norman Robert de Crevecoeur, which was appropriated by Edward I in the 13th century and became a favourite royal residence. The barbican, constructed during this time, is unique in comprising three parts, each with its own entrance: drawbridge, gateway and portcullis. The medieval keep, incorporating the Great Hall, is called the Gloriette, in honour of Edward I's wife, Queen Eleanor.

During its lifetime, Leeds Castle has been home to six medieval queens: Eleanor of Castile (wife of Edward I), Isabella (wife of Edward II), Philippa of Hainault (wife of Edward III), Joan of Navarre (wife of Philip IV of France and mother of Isabella), Catherine de Valois (wife of Henry V) and Catherine of Aragon. Not surprisingly, it's often referred to as the 'Castle of Queens, Queen of Castles'.

In the 16th century the castle was home to Catherine of Aragon, the first wife of Henry VIII, while Elizabeth I was imprisoned here for a time. Leeds Castle escaped destruction during the English Civil War when its owner, Sir Cheney Culpeper, sensibly sided with the Parliamentarians.

The castle continued as a country house through the Jacobean and Georgian eras and was extensively repaired and remodelled in Tudor style in the early 19th century (completed 1823), resulting in its appearance today. Its last private owner was an Anglo-American heiress, Lady Baillie, who purchased the castle in 1926, and restored its fabric and structure. Upon her

Leeds Castle

France to meet Francis I in 1520 at the Field of the Cloth of Gold, and a painting commemorating the glittering summit hangs in the castle. In contrast, it's also home to a unique museum displaying a collection of dog collars dating back to the late 15th century.

With 500 acres of landscaped parkland and formal gardens (Culpeper Gardens, Woodland Garden, Lady Baillie Mediterranean Terrace, etc.), a maze, grotto, waterfowl, aviaries and vineyard, plus attractions such as adventure golf and two playgrounds, Leeds Castle really does offer something for everyone.

death in 1974 she left it to the Leeds Castle Foundation, a private charitable trust whose purpose is to preserve it for the benefit of the public.

You can see reminders of all these eras, and the lives of those who occupied the castle, in the lavish rooms and the Gatehouse Museum, which takes you on a journey through over 900 years of history. It's said that Henry VIII stayed at Leeds Castle on his way to

Dining Room

Bedroom

Library

Petworth House

Address: Petworth House, Petworth, West Sussex GU28 9LR (nationaltrust.org.uk/petworth-house-and-park)

Rail: from 1h 12min to Pulborough via London Bridge or Victoria stations, then line 1 bus/taxi (7.5mi)

Road: 1h 45min (51mi) via A3 & A283

Opening Hours: 11am-5pm (but check with website)

Fees: £14.40 (child £7.20), winter £12 (child £6)

Nearby: Arundel, **Chichester**, South Downs National Park, Stanstead Park, West Dean Gardens

Food & Drink

• **Petworth Café:** Located in the former servants' hall and offering the usual National Trust range of food and drinks (10am-5pm, £).

• **The Star:** Historic Fuller's pub in Market Square, serving their range of excellent ales and tasty food, plus a special menu devoted to pie and mash (01798-368114, 11am/noon-10/11pm, £).

Set within the South Downs in West Sussex, Petworth House is a late 17th-century (Grade I listed) manor house and estate, close to the town of Petworth (51 miles from London). The site was previously occupied by a fortified manor house built by Henry de Percy, 1st Baron Percy (1273–1314), from which the 13th-century chapel and undercroft survive and are incorporated into the current house. For centuries the house and estate was the southern home of the powerful Percy family, Earls of Northumberland, but since 1750 it's been owned by the prominent Wyndham family (descendants of the Percys). The current house was rebuilt in 1688 – as

an English 'Versailles' to rival the palaces of Europe – and was altered again in the 1870s to a design by architect Anthony Salvin. The estate was given to the National Trust in

Petworth House & Park (above)

What makes Petworth unique is the merging of its art and magnificent interiors, such as the Carved Room – with splendid wood carvings by Grinling Gibbons and a superb copy of Holbein's portrait of Henry VIII – and the Grand Staircase, which features murals on the ceilings and walls by Louis Laguerre. Treasures abound throughout the house, from a 15th-century manuscript of Chaucer's *Canterbury Tales*, created just 30 years after the original, to the earliest English terrestrial globe in existence (1592) by Emery Molyneux.

1947, although the current Lord Egremont and his family continue to live in the south wing of the house.

Petworth House lacks the visual splendour of other stately homes but makes up for it with its superb art collection (see box) which was created by George Wyndham, 3rd Earl of Egremont (1751-1837), and contains no less than 19 paintings by his friend J.M.W. Turner and works by Rembrandt, Titian, Bosch, Van Dyck, Reynolds, Gainsborough, Blake and Flaxman. The paintings and sculptures are displayed as they were when the third Earl lived at Petworth, during a period that became known as its 'Golden Age'. In stark contrast to the grandeur of the state rooms, the atmospheric servants' quarters and historic kitchens offer a tantalising glimpse of life 'below stairs'.

The Petworth estate extends to over 700 acres of rolling hills and ancient trees, including an expansive deer park, landscaped by Lancelot 'Capability' Brown, containing the largest herd of fallow deer in England. There's also a 30-acre woodland garden, known as the Pleasure Ground, with an Ionic Rotunda dating from 1766 and an early 18th-century Doric Temple.

Before leaving, allow an hour or two to explore charming Petworth town, one of the UK's leading antiques centres, boasting some 25 antiques outlets, along with some outstanding cafés and restaurants.

Marble Hall

Carved Room

Petworth Town

Polesden Lacey

Address: Polesden Lacey, Great Bookham, Dorking, Surrey KT23 4PZ (nationaltrust.org.uk/polesden-lacey)

Rail: from 52min to Bookham via Waterloo station, then walk (2mi) or taxi

Road: 1h 30min (29mi) via A3

Opening Hours: 11am-5pm, garden 10am-5pm (but check website)

Fees: £13.60 (child £6.80)

Nearby: Dorking, Leatherhead, **Surrey Hills AONB**

A delightful 'Edwardian' mansion and estate at Great Bookham, Surrey (29 miles from London), on the North Downs, Polesden Lacey is one of the National Trust's most popular properties. An earlier Regency house – built by celebrated builder Thomas Cubitt – was expanded and extensively remodelled in 1906 by Margaret 'Maggie' Greville (1863-1942), a prominent Edwardian hostess, and her husband Captain Ronald Greville MP, who died in 1908, just before their vision of Polesden Lacey was completed.

The couple filled the house with fine paintings, furniture, porcelain and silver,

Polesden Lacey

which is displayed in the reception rooms and galleries as it was at the time of Maggie's celebrated house parties. The (illegitimate) daughter of brewing magnate William McEwan, she entertained lavishly and had a very impressive guest list, from Edward VII to Winston Churchill.

The Duke and Duchess of York (future George VI and Queen Elizabeth) spent part of their honeymoon there in 1923, when Elizabeth described Polesden Lacey as a 'delicious house'.

Currently there are some 15 showrooms open to the public, which are beautifully decorated and contain a splendid collection of art and antiques, including portraits by Raeburn and Reynolds, Dutch Old Masters, sparkling Fabergé objects and an impressive reredos by Edward Pearce (from St Matthew Friday Street church in London) in the entrance hall. From the stunning décor in the glittering gold Saloon to state-of-the-art conveniences, such as Maggie's personal lift, it's clear that no expense was spared when Charles Mewès and Arthur Davies – the team behind the Ritz Hotel – renovated the house.

Polesden Lacey was left to the National Trust by Mrs Greville in 1942 – including her collection of over 7,500 items – in memory of her father, William

McEwan (1827-1913 – she was his sole heir). There was a serious fire in 1960, which caused damage but not serious loss, and the house was later restored and renovated. Unlike many National Trust houses, there's little in the way of 'below stairs' rooms on view to the public, as many of the original servants' quarters are used by the Trust as part of their regional offices.

The extensive 1,400-acre estate includes a walled rose garden (boasting over 2,000 roses), lawns and ancient woodland, with some beautiful landscaped walks offering fabulous views over the surrounding rolling hills. One unusual garden 'feature' is the tomb of Mrs Greville, partly protected by high hedges, located in a topiary niche between the house and the walled garden.

Just four miles southeast, **Dorking** (see page 180) has a good selection of restaurants and pubs, and is one of southern England's best towns for antique collectors.

Food & Drink

• **Cowshed Coffee Shop & Granary Café:** With an in-house coffee shop (snacks) and café (hot lunches) with alfresco seating, you're spoilt for choice at Polesden Lacey (10am-5pm, £).

• **The Old House:** Popular Young's pub in Dorking with lots of history (parts date from the 14th century), serving fine ales and delicious homemade fare (01306-889664, noon-11pm, Mon 3-11pm, Sun noon-8pm, £-££)

Gold Saloon

Entrance Hall

Rose Garden

Waddesdon Manor

Address: Waddesdon Manor, Waddesdon, Aylesbury, Bucks HP18 0JH (waddesdon.org.uk)

Rail: from 54min to Aylesbury via Marylebone station, then shuttle bus, 16 bus or taxi (6mi)

Road: 2h 5min (61mi) via M25 & A41

Opening Hours: late Mar-Oct, grounds Wed-Sun 10am-5pm, house Wed-Fri noon-4pm, Sat-Sun 11am-4pm (see website for more information)

Fees: house & grounds £21 (child £11.50), grounds £11 (child £5.50).

Nearby: Aylesbury, Bicester, **Bletchley Park**, **Chilterns**, **Oxford**

Food & Drink

• **Manor Restaurant:** Set within the old servants' hall, the Manor offers a full menu with options for breakfast, lunch/Sunday lunch and traditional afternoon tea (01296-820414, 10am-5pm, ££).

• **Stables Café:** Appealing in-house café with courtyard seating, serving club sandwiches, burgers, soups and cakes (10am-5pm, £).

A country mansion house in the village of Waddesdon, Buckinghamshire, Grade I listed Waddesdon Manor is located in the Aylesbury Vale, seven miles west of Aylesbury (61 miles from London). One of the National Trust's most visited properties, it was built in the Neo-Renaissance style of a French chateau between 1874 and 1889 for Baron Ferdinand de Rothschild (1839–1898), for whom it was both a weekend residence for grand entertaining and a showcase for his amazing collection.

Baron Ferdinand was fascinated by 18th-century France and employed a French architect, the wonderfully named Gabriel-Hippolyte Destailleur, who created rooms using wall panels recycled from Parisian houses of the 1700s. In the Green Boudoir the panels are carved with dragons, butterflies and monkeys imitating humans, while the mirrors and marble of the Dining Room evoke a mini Versailles. Here, the richly decorated table is set for a party of 24, just as it was in the Baron's day, when 400 pieces of Sèvres porcelain were used to serve 24 people; a gift from King Louis XV to an Austrian prince in 1766, it was used by the family until the '80s. Another highlight in the East

Waddesdon Manor

Gallery is a marvellous musical automaton elephant (dating from 1774), whose parts move while it plays.

The house is packed with 18th-century French objects of exceptional quality and history. In the tower drawing room there's a delicate writing table made for Queen Marie-Antoinette, along with a carpet from the chapel in the Palace of Versailles. Above the fireplace is a vase in the shape of a ship made by the Royal Sèvres porcelain factory – only ten examples exist and Waddesdon has three of them. In contrast, Ferdinand's private sitting room is displayed exactly as it was in the 1890s, crowded but cosy, with old furniture, small treasures, flowers, family photographs and paintings by Reynolds, Gainsborough and Romney.

The last member of the Rothschild family to own Waddesdon was James de Rothschild (1878–1957), who bequeathed the house, its contents and 120 acres of grounds to the National Trust.

The gardens and park were laid out by the French landscape architect Elie Lainé, with mature trees, elaborate flower beds and artificial rock formations. Today, the spectacular (Grade I listed) grounds are lined with beautiful blooms, fine trees and elegant sculptures. Art is an important ingredient, and the fountains to the north and south of the house include sculptures of Pluto and Proserpina, originally made for the Dukes of Parma in Italy. Other highlights include the carpet beds, in which masses of tiny plants are used to create a living mosaic, and the beautifully restored cast iron aviary (erected in 1889), home to some rare and endangered birds, enclosed by intricate tiered ribbon bedding.

Red Saloon

Study

Morning Room

RHS Wisley, Surrey (see page 140)

5.
Parks, Gardens & Nature Reserves

Aplethora of beautiful green spaces, parks and gardens are within easy reach of London, in addition to the grounds belonging to stately homes mentioned in **Chapter 4**. Those featured below include magnificent Claremont Landscape Garden and Painshill Park in Surrey; lovely Leonardslee Gardens in West Sussex and historic Wrest Park Gardens in Bedfordshire; world-famous RHS Wisley (Surrey) and Sissinghurst Castle Garden (Kent); and the tranquil nature reserves of Elmley and Rainham Marshes.

Note that parks and gardens often have restricted opening times, particularly in winter (when many are closed). If you're planning to visit a number of parks and gardens (or stately homes - see **Chapter 4**) owned or managed by the National Trust and/or English Heritage, it may be worthwhile joining the relevant organisation.

Claremont Landscape Garden

Address: Claremont Landscape Garden, Portsmouth Road, Esher, Surrey KT10 9JG (nationaltrust.org.uk/claremont-landscape-garden)

Rail: from 30min to Esher via Waterloo station, then 715 bus/taxi/walk (2mi)

Road: 50min (19mi) via A3

Opening Times: 10am-4/6pm (depending on the season – see website)

Fees: £10.50 (child £5.25)

Nearby: **Chessington**, Hampton Court Palace, **Painshill**, Surrey Hills AONB

Situated just outside Esher in Surrey, 19 miles from London, Claremont is one of the earliest surviving English landscape gardens. Now Grade I listed, it was created to complement Claremont House and has retained much of its original 18th-century design. The first house was built in 1708 by Sir John Vanbrugh, designer of Blenheim Palace and Castle Howard. In 1714 it was purchased from Vanbrugh by Thomas Pelham-Holles, 1st Duke of Newcastle, who made it his bolthole for the next 50 years; after his death in 1768, the duke's widow sold Claremont to Lord Robert Clive (of India). Clive hired Lancelot 'Capability' Brown and Henry Holland to build a Palladian mansion to replace the older house, and the current incarnation of Claremont House was completed in 1774 (now a private school).

In 1816 Claremont was purchased by the British Nation as a wedding present for George IV's daughter Princess Charlotte and her husband Prince Leopold of Saxe-Coburg. Leopold's niece Queen Victoria was a frequent visitor to Claremont, both as a child and adult.

Since its inception in 1715, the garden has been tweaked and polished by some of England's most famous landscape architects, from Vanbrugh and 'Capability' Brown to Charles Bridgeman and William Kent until, by 1727, it was described as 'the noblest of any in Europe'. Bridgeman's contribution (c 1725) was the unusual turf amphitheatre, carved into a hill overlooking the lake. It formed the centrepiece of an annual event called the Claremont *Fête champêtre*, when hundreds of visitors descended on the estate (usually in costume – each year had a different theme) to enjoy four days of music, theatre and fireworks. Some ten years later, William Kent began the transformation to a more 'natural' landscape style.

View to Belvedere Tower

Claremont changed hands several more times and by 1930 was empty and marked for demolition, but was saved by the governors of (what is now) Claremont Fan Court School. In 1949, the National Trust acquired 50 acres of the estate from the school and set about restoring the gardens. Today, some 300 years after it was first planted, Claremont Landscape Garden is once again a glorious retreat, featuring a serpentine lake, an island with a pavilion, Bridgeman's amphitheatre, a grotto, a camellia terrace, bowling green, nine-pin alley, and numerous viewpoints and vistas. There's also a Victorian thatched cottage, where children can dress up in period costumes.

In 1996 the school celebrated the National Trust's centenary by opening the 281-year-old Belvedere Tower, which was previously closed to visitors. Designed by Vanbrugh as a retreat for the Duke of Newcastle, who would use it to gaze at the stars – and keep an eye

on his neighbours – the tower is unusual in that what appear to be windows are actually bricks painted black and white.

Claremont Landscape Garden is open year round and offers a delicious respite from the stresses of everyday life, just as it did for dukes and princesses in bygone days.

Claremont House

Elmley National Nature Reserve

Address: Elmley National Nature Reserve, Elmley, Isle of Sheppey, Kent ME12 3RW (elmleynaturereserve.co.uk)

Rail: from 54min to Sittingbourne (change for Swale, 11min) via Cannon Street, St Pancras International and Victoria stations, then 2mi walk or arrange collection (07582-414585)

Road: 1h 30min (56mi) via A2 & M2

Opening Times: 9am-4/5pm, closed Tue (depending on the time of year)

Fees: no entrance fee as such, but you're requested to pay £5 per car

Nearby: Faversham, Sittingbourne, **Rochester**

O n the southern side of the Isle of Sheppey in Kent (56 miles from London), Elmley is the largest bird reserve in England and the only independent National Nature Reserve in the UK. It's also a family-run farm

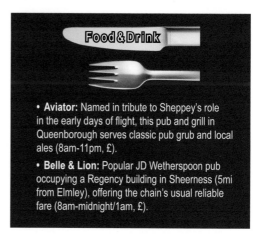

Food & Drink

- **Aviator:** Named in tribute to Sheppey's role in the early days of flight, this pub and grill in Queenborough serves classic pub grub and local ales (8am-11pm, £).
- **Belle & Lion:** Popular JD Wetherspoon pub occupying a Regency building in Sheerness (5mi from Elmley), offering the chain's usual reliable fare (8am-midnight/1am, £).

– at Elmley, conservation and agriculture go hand in hand, with grazing cattle and sheep helping to maintain the marshland for wildlife. At 3,200 acres, it's a vast wilderness, with an abundance of peaceful meadows, marshland and waterways, big skies and wonderful wildlife, providing a truly inspirational escape.

Elmley is an internationally important freshwater wetland, renowned for attracting significant numbers of over-wintering and breeding birds, plus hares, water voles, rare invertebrates and flora. Its extensive freshwater habitat lies alongside the expanses of salt marsh and mudflats of the Swale – a sea channel separating Sheppey from mainland Kent – making the reserve a refuge and restaurant for birdlife year round.

Waders and wildfowl arrive in their tens of thousands between January and March – particularly when there's a cold spell in northwest Europe – while the grazing marsh is interspersed with reed beds, rough grassland strips, hay meadows and 5½ miles of sea wall, all of

which provide habitats for many terrestrial and aquatic species. On a visit to Elmley you're likely to see water birds wading in the ponds, birds of prey soaring above, hares bounding across the meadows, and an amazing variety of insects exploring the waterways and wildflowers. If you're lucky you may also spot a water vole hiding among the reeds or a grass snake basking by the pools.

Elmley is the local name for the Isle of Elmley, divided from the rest of Sheppey by a latticework of streams and water channels. In the late 19th century this tranquil backwater was an industrial village, home to the Turkey Cement Works. It closed in 1902, after which the population dwindled and nature reclaimed the land.

Visitors can park up and use their cars as a hide – even from the car park the views are spectacular – or walk a mile along the marshes to the first hide, which overlooks a wonderful 'scrape': a shallow pool where avocet breed and numerous other birds drop in from the nearby mudflats. There are walking trails around the reserve and three further hides to discover, two overlooking pools that can be filled with thousands of

wading birds and another in a remote corner of the island. If you want to stay overnight on the reserve there are cottages and shepherd's huts for rent.

European Lapwing

Hare

Barn Owl

Epping Forest

ℹ️

Suggested start: Chingford railway station, Chingford, E4 6AL (visiteppingforest.org)

Rail: around 27min to Chingford via Liverpool Street station or 35-45 minutes to various Central Line tube stations via Oxford Circus station

Road: 45min (19mi) to Chingford via the North Circular & A406

Opening Times: unrestricted access

Fees: none

Nearby: Brentwood, Chelmsford, Enfield, Harlow, Romford

A 5,900-acre area of ancient woodland, Epping Forest straddles the border between Greater London and Essex, from Forest Gate in the south to Epping in the north, lying on a ridge between the river valleys of the Lea and Roding. The forest contains areas of woodland, grassland, heath, rivers, bogs and

Queen Elizabeth's Hunting Lodge

ponds; its elevation and thin gravelly soil (the result of glaciation) made it unsuitable for agriculture, saving it from cultivation. It's thought Epping became a royal forest in the 12th century. It's now managed by the City of London Corporation, and includes an area of 4,270 acres, designated as a Site of Special Scientific Interest and a Special Area of Conservation with national and international importance. The forest is a wonderfully varied environment, comprising over 50 distinct habitats, and is home to over 50,000 ancient pollarded trees as well as 100 lakes and ponds.

> Epping Forest is a long ribbon of wilderness, approximately 12 miles long north to south but no more than two and a half miles from east to west at its widest point.

The forest encompasses an abundance of ancient towns, villages and hamlets – each with its own unique personality, history and attractions – all connected by a network of footpaths and bridleways that crisscross the district, passing through woods and fields and along paths that have been well trodden for centuries. Overlapping the district's western boundary are the green lungs and waterways of the linear Lee Valley Park, while to the east lies the Roding Valley Meadows Nature Reserve – at 160 acres, it's the largest surviving water meadow in Essex, rich in species, with a fabulous display of wildflowers and wonderful mosaic of habitats.

There are a number of gateways to Epping Forest but a good one for newcomers is Chingford. The station is a few minutes' walk from a popular stretch of the forest, where there are numerous trails to explore. It's also close to Queen Elizabeth's Hunting Lodge (free). Located next to the visitor centre (one of four in the forest), the lodge was built by Henry VIII in 1543 and renovated for Queen Elizabeth in 1589. Neither the timber-framed building – a unique example of its kind – nor the forest which encircles it has changed much in the last five centuries. The former lodge is now a museum, featuring a Tudor kitchen, an interactive Tudor fashion display and some spectacular views.

The lodge overlooks Chingford Plain, a beautiful melange of lush grassland and shaded woodland, while a short distance to the east is Connaught Water, one of the most popular lakes in Epping Forest, with a wide variety of wildlife and a circular walk. If you want to explore further, you can pick up a brochure for walks such as the Willow Trail, which takes in Fairmead to the north.

Food & Drink

- **Brewers Fayre Royal Forest:** Family pub/restaurant in Ranger's Road, Chingford, serving classic pub fare (Mon-Sat noon-10.30/11pm, £).
- **The Larder at Butlers Retreat:** Café located in a historic restored barn offering views over Chingford Plain, serving everything from breakfast to lunch, coffee and cake to afternoon tea (9am-4/5pm, £).

Leonardslee Gardens

Address: Leonardslee Gardens, Brighton Road, Lower Beeding, Horsham, West Sussex RH13 6PP (leonardsleegardens.co.uk)

Rail: from 51min to Horsham via Victoria station, then bus 17/taxi (4.5mi)

Road: 1h 30min (50mi) via M23 & A23

Opening Times: Apr-Oct 10am-6pm, Nov-Mar 10am-4pm

Fees: £12.50 (child £6.50), payment by card only

Nearby: Crawley, High Weald AONB, Horsham, South Downs National Park

One of the finest woodland gardens in England, Leonardslee Gardens (Grade I listed) at Lower Beeding, near Horsham in West Sussex (50 miles from London), are a rare treat. The 240-acre estate was established in 1801 by Charles George Beauclerk, and takes its name from the lea or valley of St Leonard's Forest, one of the ancient forests of the High Weald, gifted by Charles II to his physician Sir Edward Greaves. The estate was acquired by Victorian plant collector Sir Edmund Loder (in 1889), who planted extensive collections of rhododendrons and azaleas, along with many tree species.

Food & Drink

• **Clocktower Café:** At the top of the gardens, the Clocktower offers a wide range of self-service refreshments, including gluten-free and vegan options, plus a farm shop selling goodies to take away (10am-6pm, £).

• **Courtyard Café:** This on-site café offers a similar range of drinks and food to the Clocktower above, plus a bar in summer (10am-6pm, £).

He also introduced a large amount of exotic flora, as well as some equally exotic animals: gazelles, beavers, kangaroos and wallabies (the descendants of which remain today). Other additions included a sandstone rock garden built by Victorian landscapers James Pulham and Sons around 1890, as well as a rock mound with caves that was constructed to house mouflon (wild sheep) and has now been taken over by the wallabies.

The gardens are overlooked by Leonardslee House (Grade II listed), built in the 19th century in Italianate style.

The 200-acre gardens – a combination of parkland, lawn and forest – are set in a steep-sided sheltered valley that contains a series of seven man-made ponds, some of which provided power for the Wealden iron industry in the 17th century. Leonardslee is home to many rare trees and shrubs and is particularly noted for its magnificent spring displays of rhododendrons, azaleas, camellias, magnolias and bluebells, with the flowering season reaching its peak in May.

The gardens were sold by the Loder family in 2010 and closed to the public. They were acquired in 2017 by entrepreneur Penny Streeter of the Benguela Collection, who comprehensively restored the gardens and reopened them in April 2019.

Visitors can explore a wide range of features, including two alpine glasshouses, the aforementioned rock garden, a unique museum called Beyond the Doll's

House – a miniaturised version of an Edwardian estate – plus the colony of wallabies, over 100 free-roaming deer (sika, axis and fallow) and huge carp in the ponds. There are numerous walking trails throughout the estate, which is home to an abundance of wildlife, including foxes, rabbits, grey squirrels,

Wallaby

badgers, weasels, stoats, shrews and voles, along with a plethora of bird species, including green woodpeckers, herons, kingfishers, mandarin ducks, nuthatches and tree creepers.

The gardens have a number of cafés and other dining options (see **Food & Drink** box) and there's no shortage of places to enjoy the perfect picnic.

Painshill Park

Address: Painshill Park, Portsmouth Rd, Cobham, Surrey KT11 1JE (painshill.co.uk)

Rail: from 30min to Cobham & Stoke d'Abernon via Waterloo station, then bus/taxi/walk (2mi)

Road: 50min (22mi) via A3

Opening Times: park 10am-4/6pm (check website)

Fees: £8.80 (child £4.60)

Nearby: Chessington, **Claremont**, **Dorking**, the Medicine Garden, **RHS Wisley**, Surrey Hills AONB

An award-winning 18th-century landscape park in Cobham, Surrey (just 22 miles from London), Painshill (Grade I listed) is one of the finest remaining examples of its kind, extending to over 158 acres along the winding River Mole. The park was created between 1738 and 1773 by the Hon. Charles Hamilton MP (1704-1786), who embarked upon two Grand Tours across Europe before acquiring land at Painshill. Inspired by the Renaissance art he'd seen on his travels, Hamilton created a sequence of breath-taking vistas – dubbed the 'natural style' or the English landscape garden – which form living works of art, into which he placed follies for dramatic effect.

The central feature is a 14-acre serpentine lake, dotted with several islands and spanned by bridges and a causeway. The water for the lake (and the plantings) was pumped from the River Mole by a 19th-century beam engine powered by a water wheel. Hamilton enhanced the views of hills and lake by carefully planting woods, avenues and specimen trees to create glorious panoramas – the Great Cedar is 120ft (37m) high and thought to be the largest cedar of Lebanon in Europe. He also added a number of discreet environments, including an amphitheatre, water meadow and alpine valley.

Hamilton adored follies (small decorative buildings) and added them to his vistas to act as focal points or delightful devices to be discovered in the landscape. Painshill's follies included a crystal grotto, the 'ruins' of a Gothic abbey, a Roman mausoleum and a Turkish tent. All still exist – or have been recreated – for modern-day visitors to enjoy.

The house built by Hamilton has long since been demolished. He eventually ran out of money and sold the estate in 1773 to Benjamin Bond Hopkins, who engaged Richard Jupp to rebuild the house in a different location; it was extended in the 19th century by Decimus Burton and is now a Grade II* listed (private) building. The estate passed through a succession of owners until in 1948, it was divided up and sold in separate lots. The park, as such, soon disappeared and its features fell into decay. The remaining 160 acres (there were originally 200) were purchased in 1980 by Elmbridge Borough Council, which has undertaken a programme of continual restoration ever since.

The original Painshill Park was intended to take visitors along a specific route where they could experience a variety of moods, just as Hamilton would have done on his Grand Tours. Thus the winding paths guide you on a journey of discovery as you explore the mystical follies, enjoy captivating views across the landscape and immerse yourself in Hamilton's Renaissance-inspired vision. It's a special voyage through one man's extraordinary imagination translated into a natural wonderland.

Food & Drink

- **Mr Hamilton's Tea Room:** Painshill's café offering breakfast, brunch and lunch, with alfresco seating and expansive views (10am-4/6pm, £).
- **Plough Inn:** Cosy country pub on Downside Road with stripped floors, armchairs, open fire, beer garden and gastro menu (01932-862244, 11am-11pm/midnight, £-££).

Grotto

Water Wheel

Ruins of 'Gothic Abbey'

Rainham Marshes Nature Reserve

Address: Rainham Marshes Nature Reserve, New Tank Hill Road, Purfleet, South Ockendon, Essex RM19 1SZ (rspb.org.uk/reserves-and-events/reserves-a-z/rainham-marshes)

Rail: from 30min to Purfleet via Fenchurch Street station, then walk (15min)

Road: 35min (16mi) via A13

Opening Times: Feb-Oct 9.30am-5pm, Nov-Jan 9.30am-4.30pm (see website)

Fees: £6 (£3 child)

Nearby: Dagenham, Grays, Purfleet, Rainham

Rainham Marshes RSPB (Royal Society for the Protection of Birds) Nature Reserve is a 1,000-acre wetland on the upper Thames Estuary (16 miles from London) and a magnet for bird lovers and nature

Food & Drink

- **Rainham Marshes Café:** Hot drinks and food, including vegan/vegetarian options, with splendid views over the marshes (10am to 4/4.30pm, £).
- **Royal Hotel:** Popular hotel on the Thames in Purfleet offering all the pub favourites, including traditional Sunday roast (lunch from noon, £).

enthusiasts. The reserve is one of the few ancient medieval landscapes remaining in the London area, comprising the largest area of wetland in the upper region of the Thames Estuary. Previously used as a firing range by the Ministry of Defence, the marshes were closed to the public for over 100 years. They were acquired by the RSPB in 2000 and opened in 2006. The RSPB has transformed the reserve into a unique habitat with a wide variety of wetland plants. It's simply teeming with wildlife, from birds and mammals – the reserve is home to one of the country's most dense populations of water vole – to insects (dragonflies and butterflies abound) and reptiles.

Needless to say, the stars are the reserve's innumerable birds, which include breeding waders, such as redshank and snipe, as well as large numbers of wintering wildfowl, finches and birds of prey. Among the main attractions are avocet, Cetti's warbler, lapwing, little egret, marsh harriers, bearded tits, peregrine, wigeon and golden

The reserve is a 20-minute walk from Purfleet station. Turn right out of the station along London Road and left to join the Thameside path just before the Royal Hotel – look for the brown tourist information signs – then turn right on the waterfront to follow the river wall path and cross the bridge over the Mar Dyke to the visitor centre.

plover. Each season brings a different experience. In spring, the air is filled with birdsong as birds compete to establish territories and attract a mate, while in summer you'll see fledglings making their first venture into the outside world. Autumn brings large movements of migrating birds – some heading south to a warmer climate, while others seek refuge in the UK from the cold Arctic winter – and in winter there are large flocks of wildfowl gathering to feed or forming large roosts at dusk to keep warm.

The reserve organises regular events for bird enthusiasts, from novice to expert, throughout the year, including guided birding walks, dawn chorus walks, winter spectacle birding events and a bird-watching club for children. There's also an innovative visitor centre, with huge picture windows overlooking the marshes, and hides affording expansive views of the reserve. The visitor centre is packed with environmentally-friendly features and boasts a number of prestigious architectural awards. With around 2½ miles of trails, a children's adventure play area, wildlife garden, marshland discovery zone, shop and café, Rainham Marshes Nature Reserve offers something for everyone, from families to walkers to wildlife enthusiasts. It's the ultimate big sky escape from crowded London.

Curlew

Visitor Centre

Kingfisher

Vole

RHS Wisley

Address: RHS Wisley, Wisley Lane, Wisley, Woking, Surrey GU23 6QB (rhs.org.uk/gardens/wisley)

Rail: from 23min to West Byfleet or Woking via Waterloo station, then taxi (4 or 7mi)

Road: 55min (26mi) via M4 & M25

Opening Times: spring/summer Mon-Fri 10am-6pm, Sat-Sun 9am-6pm (closes 4.30pm in winter)

Fees: £14.50 (£7.25)

Nearby: Claremont, **Dorking**, Guildford, Leatherhead, **Painshill**, Surrey Hills AONB

A Garden for all Seasons

Seasonal highlights include a carpet of crocuses and magnificent displays of magnolias, rhododendrons and fruit blossom in spring; summer's glorious roses (e.g. the Bowes-Lyon Rose Garden), meadow flowers, and colourful mixed borders; autumn's bountiful harvest and wonderful golden colours; and winter's wonderland of evergreens, berries, vivid stems and frost-sparkled walks.

The historic home of the Royal Horticultural Society, RHS Wisley in Surrey (26 miles from London) is one of the UK's best-loved gardens – indeed, it's one of the finest gardens in the world. The RHS has been the guardian of Wisley since 1903 when it was gifted to them by its last owner. Back then, only a small part of the 60-acre estate was cultivated as a garden, the remainder being wooded farmland. The original garden was the creation of George Fergusson Wilson, businessman, scientist, inventor and keen gardener, and a former treasurer of the Society. In 1878 he purchased the site and established the 'Oakwood experimental garden', with the objective of making 'difficult plants grow successfully'. Wilson acquired a reputation for his collections of lilies, gentians, Japanese irises, primulas and water plants. After his death in 1902, Oakwood and the adjoining Glebe Farm were bought by Sir Thomas Hanbury (1832-1907), who donated the estate in trust to the RHS in perpetuity.

Today, 240-acre Wisley is the RHS's flagship garden, showcasing the widest range of gardening styles and techniques, and home to some of the largest plant collections in the world. In addition to numerous decorative gardens, several glasshouses and an extensive arboretum, it includes small-scale 'model gardens' designed to show visitors what they can achieve in their own plots, and a trials field where new cultivars are assessed. The gardens are also home to the iconic Arts and Crafts style laboratory building (Grade II listed), built in 1916.

There are 25 different gardens on view at Wisley, including a walled garden, cottage garden, rose garden,

Laboratory Building

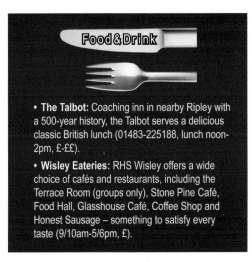

Food&Drink

- **The Talbot:** Coaching inn in nearby Ripley with a 500-year history, the Talbot serves a delicious classic British lunch (01483-225188, lunch noon-2pm, £-££).

- **Wisley Eateries:** RHS Wisley offers a wide choice of cafés and restaurants, including the Terrace Room (groups only), Stone Pine Café, Food Hall, Glasshouse Café, Coffee Shop and Honest Sausage – something to satisfy every taste (9/10am-5/6pm, £).

conifers, while the newest (2017) is the Exotic Garden, filled with palms, banana plants and large vibrant tropical blossoms.

The Lindley Library contains a world-renowned gardening collection and is open to all for browsing, research and inspiration, while visitors can purchase plants from the plant centre and books, gifts, home accessories and food items from the gift shop. The garden offers no less than six cafés and restaurants or you can bring a picnic. Wisley is also a backdrop for sculpture, craft fairs, and a programme of diverse leisure courses in gardening, photography and art throughout the year. Whether you have an estate or a window box, you're sure to find inspiration at Wisley.

mixed borders and a bonsai walk. The Glasshouse features plants from tropical, moist temperate and dry temperate habitats, while the Woodland Garden (Battleston Hill) is at its most beautiful in spring, when its winding paths are bordered with camellias, magnolias, rhododendrons, hydrangeas and azaleas. One of the oldest gardens (constructed 1910-12) is the naturalistic Rock Garden, showcasing alpine plants with dwarf

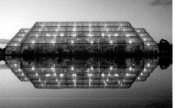

Glasshouse

The Sculpture Park

Address: The Sculpture Park, corner of Jumps and Tilford Road, Churt, near Farnham, Surrey GU10 2LH (thesculpturepark.com)

Rail: from 55min to Farnham via Waterloo station, then no 19 bus to Churt (20min) and taxi/walk 1½mi

Road: 1h 15min (44mi) via M25 & A3

Opening Times: daily 10am-5pm

Fees: £10 (child £5)

Nearby: Farnham, Guildford, South Downs National Park, Surrey Hills AONB, **Watts Gallery**, Winkworth Arboretum

Food & Drink

• **Bel & the Dragon:** Country inn with 18 rooms close to the park, with a bar/restaurant and large garden, serving classic British cuisine (01428-605799, lunch noon-3pm, £).

• **The Botanist Farnham:** Popular bar/restaurant in nearby Farnham (6mi) with live music, offering modern European food (01252-718089, Mon-Thu 11am-midnight, Fri-Sun 9.30am-midnight/1am, £).

Possibly the most extensive display of 20th-century, modern and contemporary sculpture in the world, the Sculpture Park in Churt, Surrey (44 miles from London), is home to over 650 sculptures by more than 300 artists. Opened to the public in 2003, the collection is set within an enchanting 10-acre arboretum and water gardens, which have been sympathetically landscaped and planted with thousands of bulbs, plants and specimen trees. The design takes advantage of the contours of the rolling Surrey Hills, which has resulted in the perfect backdrop for the display of artworks. With over two miles of paths meandering through mixed heathland and woodland in a natural valley – enhanced by three lakes fed by two natural springs – the Sculpture Park is one of Surrey's hidden gems.

The park is teeming with flora and fauna, which changes through the seasons, as do the sculptures themselves. In spring (when the luxuriant rhododendrons are in bloom) and summer you'll find yourself lost in a kaleidoscope of lush gardens, while autumn makes way for a sea of reds and oranges followed by the (sculptural) bare trees of winter which allow you to see more of the vast exhibition, spotting sculptures from afar while still managing to lose yourself in the depths of the woodland. There's also a small

indoor gallery where more works can be viewed.

Visitors should allow two to four hours for a visit, as with ten acres and over two miles of trails the park is larger than many anticipate. There's no café but you can bring a picnic and there are some excellent restaurants close by (see **Food & Drink**). There's also a wealth of other attractions in the surrounding Surrey Hills Area of Outstanding Natural Beauty (AONB), offering an abundance of beautiful landscapes and walks, including the Devil's Punch Bowl, Frensham Ponds, the ruins of Waverley Abbey, Bourne Wood (a popular film and TV location) and the 800-acre Thursley National Nature Reserve.

The eclectic collection of sculptures encompasses a huge variety of styles – abstract, animal, figurative, garden, indoor, kinetic, nude and water features – while the materials employed include bronze, ceramic, glass, lead, slate, granite, wood, stone, marble, copper and steel. Most of the artworks are for sale.

Sissinghurst Castle Garden

Address: Sissinghurst Castle Garden, Biddenden Road, near Cranbrook, Kent TN17 2AB (nationaltrust.org.uk/sissinghurst-castle-garden)

Rail: from 55min to Staplehurst via London Cannon Street, Charing Cross and St Pancras International stations, then line 5 bus/taxi (5mi)

Road: 1h 30min (62mi) via A2

Opening Times: Mar-Oct, garden 11am-5.30pm, estate dawn to dusk (but check website)

Fees: £13.80 (child £6.90)

Nearby: High Weald AONB, **Leeds Castle**

Created by Vita Sackville-West (1892-1962) and her author-diplomat husband Sir Harold Nicolson (1886-1968), Sissinghurst Castle Garden (Grade I listed) in the Weald of Kent (62 miles from London) is one of the most

Following Vita's death in 1962, the estate was given to the National Trust by her son Nigel Nicolson. His mother had been opposed to the idea when it was suggested in 1954 ('It is bad enough to have lost my Knole but they shan't take Sissinghurst from me') but Nicolson felt it was the best way to preserve it, and the NT took over Sissinghurst in 1967.

celebrated gardens in the world. The site of Sissinghurst has been occupied since at least the Middle Ages. The present-day buildings began as a manor house built in the 1530s by Sir John Baker, whose daughter Cecily married Thomas Sackville, 1st Earl of Dorset, an ancestor of Vita Sackville-West. By the 18th century the Baker family's fortunes had waned, and the house was leased to the government as a prisoner-of-war camp during the Seven Years' War with France (1756-1763). The prisoners referred to Sissinghurst as the *chateau*, which was how the name Castle came to be adopted. During the 19th century the Elizabethan house was partly demolished and all that remain from that era are the Tower – once the gatehouse and later Vita's bolthole – the West Range, South Cottage, Priest's House and Great Barn.

Sissinghurst Castle Tower

Food & Drink

- **Restaurant & Coffee Shop:** Sissinghurst's on-site coffee shop offers a range of drinks, cakes, soup and sandwiches, while the restaurant serves tasty seasonal dishes using produce from the garden (10am-5.30pm, £).

- **The Milk House:** A former 16th-century hall house in Sissinghurst village, now a chic gastropub with a lawn terrace and delicious food, including wood-fired pizzas (01580-720200, 9am-11pm, £-££).

The estate was purchased by Sackville-West (born in nearby Knole House – see page 116) and her husband in 1930, and over the next 30 years they (along with a string of notable head gardeners) transformed a farmstead of 'squalor and slovenly disorder' into one of the world's most influential gardens, a prime example of Arts and Crafts style. Harold's architectural planning and Vita's abundant, colourful planting reflect the romance and intimacy of her poems and writings.

Today, Sissinghurst Castle Gardens are home to an internationally respected plant collection, particularly the massed ranks of old garden roses which are among the finest in the world. The design of the gardens is based on the concept of 'garden rooms' – enclosed gardens resembling outdoor rooms, each with a theme, linked by walkways – and Sissinghurst is one of the earliest examples of this gardening style. Among the individual garden rooms, the most famous and influential is the White Garden, which exemplified and popularised Gertrude Jekyll's idea of using colour themes in planting design.

The gardens take up only a fraction (5 acres) of the estate's 450 acres of beautiful Wealden countryside, which offers plenty of space to explore. You can even stay in the estate's own B&B, set in a Victorian farmhouse and offering far-reaching views across the ancient woodland or towards Vita's beloved Elizabethan tower.

Vita Sackville-West

Wrest Park Gardens

Address: Wrest Park, Silsoe, Bedfordshire MK45 4HR (english-heritage.org.uk/visit/places/wrest-park)

Rail: from 51min to Flitwick via St Pancras International station, then bus/taxi (5mi)

Road: 1h 20min (47mi) via M1

Opening Times: 10am-6pm (4pm in winter – check website for dates)

Fees: £11.50 (child £6.90)

Nearby: Bedford, **Bletchley Park**, Hitchin, **Woburn**

A country estate located in Silsoe, Bedfordshire (47 miles from London), Wrest Park consists of an outstanding restored English landscape garden originating in the 17th century, which surrounds a mansion built in the 1830s (both Grade I listed). The vast gardens showcase over three centuries of garden design, incorporating French, Dutch, Italian and English influences, and are a treat for anyone interested in horticultural history.

> Wrest House was built in 1834-39 to designs by Thomas de Grey, 2nd Earl de Grey, the first president of the Royal Institute of British Architects (RIBA). It's an almost unique example of 19th-century English architecture following the style of an 18th-century French chateau, and contains some of the earliest Rococo Revival interiors in England. There's a fascinating exhibit about the house and its owners on the ground floor, and visitors are free to explore the glittering state rooms.

For over 600 years the Wrest estate was home to one of the leading aristocratic families in the country, the de Greys, with each generation leaving its mark. The family achieved its greatest prominence when Edward IV made Edmund Grey his Lord Treasurer in 1463 and then Earl of Kent in 1465. Over 200 years later the formal gardens and the canal known as the Long Water were created by Amabel Benn, together with her son Anthony, the 11th Earl. In the early 18th century, Anthony's son (Henry, Duke of Kent), laid out what is now Wrest's most exceptional feature: its massive formal woodland garden, enclosed on three sides by canals. He employed leading architects and garden designers – including Nicholas Hawksmoor and William Kent – to create an ordered landscape of avenues ornamented with statuary and garden buildings. In 1758 Lancelot 'Capability' Brown – a leading proponent of the

Wrest House & Gardens

new English landscape style – was employed to soften the edges and remodel the park, while preserving the heart of the formal layout.

In the early 20th century, Wrest Park was, in turn, a convalescence home, an insurance company HQ and an agricultural research institute. The gardens were overlooked until, in 2006, English Heritage began an ambitious 20-year project to restore them to their pre-1917 state.

Spread over 92 acres, Wrest Park Gardens now offer a rare opportunity to explore the evolution of the English garden, from dazzling parterres and fragrant borders to sweeping vistas and woodland walks. The gardens contain a number of structural gems, including 18th-century Bowling Green House, a striking Chinese bridge and temple, and over 40 statues dotted around the grounds. (The Dairy Sculpture Gallery and the Archaeological Collections Store contain further sculptural gems.) Stroll up the Long Water to the spectacular Baroque Archer Pavilion (1709-11) with its stunning interior – the focal point of the gardens – and delight in the fancy French curves and intricate Italian geometry of the restored bedding displays. From lush greens in spring, to summer's breathtaking blooms and a kaleidoscope of autumnal reds and golds, Wrest Park really is a garden for all seasons.

Food & Drink

• **Café:** Wrest Park's on-site café is located in the delightful walled garden, offering hot and cold drinks, cakes, soups and sandwiches, using locally-sourced produce (10am-4/6pm, £).

• **Star & Garter:** Cosy 17th-century pub-restaurant in Silsoe village, serving good ales and tasty pub grub (01525-860250, lunch 11am-3pm, £).

Carousel Garden

Chinese Bridge

Long Water & Archer Pavilion

Nemesis Inferno roller coaster, Thorpe Park (see page 164)

6.
Mainly for Kids

This chapter contains ten suggestions for family days out from London with children, most of which can be reached in less than an hour by train.

Bear in mind that you need a whole day to make the most of a visit to theme parks, so try to get there as soon as the park opens. If you're going at peak times – weekends and school holidays are best avoided – you should try to mix popular and less-popular (or 'no-queue') rides. You may be able to reduce your queueing time by making reservations in advance, but this can be expensive. It's often cheaper to book tickets in advance online, rather than pay on the day. Note that some rides have age and/or height restrictions.

Bear in mind that on-site food can be poor and expensive. Where feasible we have offered off-site alternatives – or you can bring a picnic.

Bekonscot Model Village

Address: Bekonscot Model Village, Warwick Road, Beaconsfield, Bucks, HP9 2PL (bekonscot. co.uk)

Rail: from 26min to Beaconsfield via Marylebone station

Road: 55min (27mi) via A40/M40

Opening Times: Feb-Nov 10am-5.30pm (see website for exact dates)

Fees: £10.90 (child £7)

Nearby: Chilterns, Cookham, Great Missenden, High Wycombe, Oxford

Bekonscot is a riot of colour during the spring and summer, the little towns framed by thousands of bedding and herbaceous plants. The gardens contain over 3,000 shrubs and trees, many of which are of 'bonsai-style' in scale with the models – although bonsai buffs rightly point out that they're actually skilfully trimmed standard garden plants.

Opened in 1929, Bekonscot Model Village and Railway is the world's oldest model village, with finely-detailed buildings (scaled down to 1:12), an extensive railway and 1½ acres of manicured gardens. Situated 27 miles west of London in Buckinghamshire, Bekonscot was the inspiration for model villages in the UK and further afield, and is regarded as the 'grandfather' of the model village and miniature park movement. It has featured in numerous TV shows and is said to have inspired the series of *Borrowers* books by Mary Norton.

Bekonscot comprises not one but six fictional towns – Bekonscot Town, Evenlode & Epwood, Greenhaily, Hanton, Southpool and Splashyng – all stuck in an early '30s time-warp, providing a glimpse of an era when life moved at a slower and gentler pace. Each has its own character, inhabitants and features, from coal mines to castles, aerodromes to racecourses, and cable cars to windmills. In total, there are over 200 buildings and 3,000 people – look out for the Morris men in Splashyng's square and the convicts fleeing Bekonscot's police station – plus 1,000 animals, hundreds of vehicles and many animated models.

The village was created in the '20s by accountant Roland Callingham (1881-1961), who

developed his miniature empire in his large back garden, with help from his gardener, cook, maid and chauffeur. Together, they developed a model landscape portraying rural England at the time. Callingham named the village 'Bekonscot' after Beaconsfield and Ascot, and commissioned Bassett-Lowke to build an extensive Gauge 1 railway network for the project. The historic railway has been famous since 1929 as one of the largest and most complex in the UK, complete with a full-size signal box and lever frame controlling up to 12 trains simultaneously. There's also a narrow (7.25in) gauge light railway which takes full-size passengers on a ride (fee) around the village between 10.30am and 4.30pm.

Although conceived as a plaything to entertain Callingham and his guests, when Bekonscot's existence became widely known it attracted a steady stream of curious sightseers. Visitors were invited to make a donation to the Railway Benevolent Institution, and so Bekonscot became a commercial attraction. It has been run by the Church Army since 1978 and still donates large amounts of money to charity – over £5 million to date.

Food & Drink

• **The Beech House:** Cosy gastropub in Beaconsfield town, with sofas and open fires, serving Mediterranean and British dishes (01494-842166, 8am-11pm/1am, £).

• **Tea Room:** Spacious on-site tea room serving sandwiches, ice cream and hot foods, including jacket potatoes and burgers – plus a picnic area (10am-5.30pm, £).

Bluebell Railway

Address: Bluebell Railway, East Grinstead Station, Railway Approach, East Grinstead, West Sussex RH19 1EB (bluebell-railway.com)

Rail: from 59min via Victoria station

Road: 1h 30min (30mi) via A23 & A22

Opening Times: see website for timetable

Fees: all-day rover £19 (child £9.50)

Nearby: Crawley, High Weald AONB, Royal Tunbridge Wells, Sheffield Park

Food & Drink

• **Grinsteade Buffet:** The café at East Grinstead station is located in an original buffet carriage, serving hot drinks, sandwiches, a tasty ploughman's lunch, and homemade cakes and cream teas (10am-4.30pm, £).

• **Ounce & Ivy Bush:** Formerly the Radio Centre Cinema, it's now a Wetherspoon pub offering an extensive menu of drinks and pub grub (7am-midnight, £).

The Bluebell Railway is one of the best-preserved heritage lines in the country, with an exceptional collection of vintage steam locomotives and carriages. Its rolling stock includes trains from the 1880s through to the '60s, many of which came straight out of service from British Railways. More than just a museum, the Bluebell was the first preserved standard gauge, steam-operated passenger railway in the world to operate a public service, running its first train in August 1960, less than three years after the line it was using – between East Grinstead and Lewes – was closed. Not surprisingly, it's popular with film-makers, and Horsted Keynes station has appeared regularly on screen – it doubles as Downton Station in the *Downton Abbey* TV drama.

By the time steam stopped running on British mainline railways in 1968, the Bluebell had already saved a number of steam locomotives and it now has over 30 – the largest collection in the UK after the National Railway Museum in York. In addition, it has some 150 carriages and wagons, most pre-1939, one of which has been extensively modified with double doors, wheelchair lifts and an open saloon.

In March 2013, the Bluebell Railway began running to its new East Grinstead terminus station, on platform

3 of the mainline station. This was the first time in 50 years that the Bluebell Railway had a connection to the national network since the Horsted Keynes-Haywards Heath line closed in 1963. Today, the railway – managed and run largely by volunteers – operates trains on an 11-mile stretch of track between Sheffield Park and East Grinstead, with intermediate stations at Horsted Keynes and Kingscote. Dining trains (e.g. the *Sussex Belle*) operate on selected dates, including services for lunch, afternoon tea and silver-service dining, supper specials and 'rail ale' evenings.

The stations along the Bluebell Line have been restored to reflect different periods of the railway's history. Sheffield Park has a Victorian ambience, recollecting the era of the London, Brighton and South Coast Railway (1846-1922), while Horsted Keynes recalls the days of the Southern Railway from 1922 to 1948. Tranquil Kingscote has a mid-'50s vibe, while East Grinstead echoes the British Rail heyday of the '50s and '60s.

There are events year round, including collectors' fairs, murder mystery evenings and visits by 'guest' engines, as well as bespoke trips to celebrate special days or corporate events – assisted by a qualified guide. A trip on the Bluebell Line isn't just for steam buffs but is a treat for anyone interested in a time when rail travel was still an adventure.

Chessington World of Adventures

Address: Chessington World of Adventures, Leatherhead Road, Chessington KT9 2NE (chessington.com)

Rail: from 36min to Chessington South via Waterloo station, then 10m walk or taxi (½mi)

Road: 50min (17mi) via A3

Opening Times: 10am-5/6pm (but check website)

Fees: Online Saver Ticket £29.50 (check offers online)

Nearby: Epsom, Hobbledown, **Painshill**

A theme park, zoo and hotel complex, Chessington World of Adventures is located 17 miles southwest of central London. First launched as Chessington Zoo in 1931, it was originally a showcase for Reginald Stuart Goddard's collection of animals, the largest private zoo in England. The zoo is now home to over 1,000 animals, including western lowland gorillas and Sumatran tigers, although Chessington is now known for its white-knuckle rides as much as its wildlife.

The zoo is divided into several areas, including Trail of the Kings (big cats and gorillas), Penguin Bay, Amazu – which takes you into the treetops with the monkeys and macaws – and the Wanyama Village & Reserve, home to zebras and meerkats. There's also a fascinating Sea Life Centre to explore.

Chessington's history dates back to the Middle Ages. The first incarnation of Burnt Stub Mansion (aka Hocus Pocus Hall, aka Room on a Broom) was built in 1348. It was a Royalist stronghold during the English Civil War, before Oliver Cromwell's Parliamentary forces razed it to the ground. It was rebuilt at least twice and by the 18th/19th century had become a neo-Gothic Victorian family home.

The theme park was developed alongside the zoo by the Tussauds Group and when it opened in July 1987 – with just five rides – it was one of the first themed amusement parks in Britain. It now has ten themed areas and 40 rides and attractions, including long-established favourites such as the swinging Vampire coaster and the spinning Rameses Revenge, which gives riders a thorough soaking while they're suspended in mid-air.

Chessington's themes are loosely styled on a range of world cultures. Adventure Point is an English market square and Pirates' Cove a Cornish fishing village; Mexicana borrows from the Wild West, while Wild Woods resembles

Rameses Revenge

Food&Drink

• Chessington offers a wealth of cafés, restaurants and fast-food outlets, some of which can be booked online. Options include burgers, ribs, hot dogs, chicken, fish and chips, pizza, jacket potatoes, sandwiches and a range of sweet treats such as doughnuts and ice cream (10am-5/6pm, £).

Now owned by Merlin Entertainments (which merged with the Tussauds Group in 2007), Chessington has been increasingly developed into a resort destination – a British Disney – and now has two on-site hotels and a camp site. Aimed at families rather than thrill-seekers, Chessington has plenty of children's rides, from traditional carousels to movie tie-ins such as Treetop Hoppers, featuring the smash-hit animation series *Madagascar*. It also hosts seasonal events, such as Roar & Explore (special evenings at the zoo), and Howl'o'ween (spooky rides after dark).

Kobra

a town in Bavaria; the Forbidden Kingdom mirrors Egypt and Arabia, while the Land of the Tiger has an Oriental theme and Wild Asia transports you to a jungle in deepest India. Each area features flagship rides such as Dragon's Fury, Kobra, Tiger Rock, Scorpion Express and The Gruffalo River Ride Adventure.

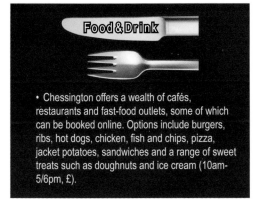

Sumatran Tiger

Sea Life

Monkey Swinger

Chislehurst Caves

Food & Drink

- **The Bickley:** Huge pub-restaurant close to the caves with a marble bar, walled garden and a roof terrace, offering excellent modern British fare (020-8468 7613, noon-11pm/midnight, £).
- **Imperial Arms Pub & Courtyard Bistro:** Friendly gastropub and bistro, offering a wide choice of wines by the glass (020-3605-7899, noon-10.30pm/midnight, £-££).

Address: Chislehurst Caves, Caveside Close, Old Hill, Chislehurst BR7 5NL (chislehurst-caves.co.uk)

Rail: from 28min to Chislehurst via Charing Cross station, then short walk

Road: 55min (13mi) via A20

Opening Times: Wed-Sun by guided tour 10am-4pm

Fees: £6 (child £4)

Nearby: Bromley, Orpington, Sidcup

The Chislehurst Caves are one of Greater London's more bizarre attractions, comprising some 25 miles of tunnels buried 100ft below the upmarket commuter town of Chislehurst (just 13 miles from central London). They aren't actually caves, but rather man-made mines, dug by hand to extract flint and chalk. It's impossible to put a precise date on them, but some experts believe the caves originated in the Neolithic (New Stone Age), around 8,000 years ago, when flint was a necessary element of weapons and tools. Flint from the caves was also used to fire the tinderboxes and flintlock guns of the 17th-19th centuries, while chalk was extracted for lime-burning and brick-making, and for use as fertiliser and in cement.

Certain features in the caves are thought by some – including the more fanciful tour guides – to be Roman workings or Druid altars, but this is, at best, speculation. The first recorded reference dates from 1250 and they were mined until the 1830s. The caves saw service as an ammunition dump for the Royal Arsenal at Woolwich during the First World War. They were used for mushroom cultivation during

the '30s, while in the Second World War they became an air raid shelter, effectively an underground town of around 15,000 people, with electric light, a chapel and a hospital. Surprisingly, only one baby was recorded as being born in the caves, appropriately named Rose Cavena Wakeman.

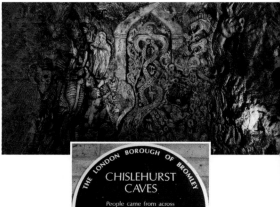

Cave Carvings

> It's cool underground – the caves are a constant 10ºC/50ºF – and tours last around 45 minutes, so dress appropriately, especially when visiting in summer. Sensible shoes are essential. You can warm up with a hot drink afterwards in the Cave Café.

The '60s saw yet another role for the caves, this time as a music venue, hosting performances by such luminaries as David Bowie, Jimi Hendrix, Pink Floyd, The Rolling Stones and Status Quo. A number of bands have made videos here and in 1974, Led Zeppelin launched their Swansong record label with a lavish party in the caves. Inevitably, the caves have also featured in television programmes, including several episodes of *Doctor Who* in the early '70s and, more recently, the BBC drama *Merlin*.

Group tours of the caves are led by enthusiastic amateur guides, and there's no lighting except for oil lamps. It makes for a spooky atmosphere and it's no surprise that Chislehurst Caves are allegedly haunted, with a number of guides and visitors claiming to have seen and heard strange things.

Legoland Windsor

Address: Legoland Windsor, Winkfield Road, Windsor, Berkshire SL4 4AY (legoland.co.uk)

Rail: from 26min to Windsor & Eton Central via Paddington and Waterloo stations, then shuttle bus (2mi)

Road: 50min (26mi) via A4 & M4

Opening Times: 10am-5pm (but check website)

Fees: Online Saver £29 (check offers) – it's cheaper to book in advance online

Nearby: Cookham, Thorpe Park, Windsor

Based on the Lego toy system – from building bricks to mini-figures – Legoland Windsor is a theme park and resort firmly focused on younger visitors. It opened in March 1996 on the old Windsor Safari Park site (26 miles from London) and was the second Legoland to launch after the original Legoland Billund in Denmark. The park was acquired by Merlin Entertainments (who also own Chessington World of Adventures – see page 154) in 2005 and has since been a huge success. It was the most visited theme park in the UK in 2017 with over 2.2 million visitors – more even than the Billund park – and the tenth most popular theme park in Europe.

Note

As with most theme parks, there are frequent complaints regarding queueing. You can reduce queueing time by buying a Q-Bot, which allows you to make ride reservations in advance. However, it's **very** expensive and most experts recommend going on a 'quiet' day.

In common with other Legolands across the world, Windsor's attractions consist of a mixture of Lego-themed rides, models and building workshops, mostly targeted at children aged between three and twelve. Child-free adults may feel out of place here and the rides are fun rather than frightening.

The park is split into 11 'lands', incorporating over 55 rides, shows and attractions, plus restaurants and shops galore. They include Miniland (a shrunken world built from Lego bricks), Duplo Valley (wet rides for younger kids), Lego City (balloons, boats and cars), Knights' Kingdom (home of The Dragon rollercoaster), Land of the Vikings (more water-based fun) and Lego Ninjago World (4D rides and a climbing wall). Some rides have minimum height requirements (35½in or 90cm rising to 43/51in or 110/130cm for some rides), and many are designed to leave you

soaking wet – so bring swimwear, towels and a change of clothes!

There's far too much to see and do in one day (even without queues), so it's advisable to plan in advance what your kids most want to experience – or plan a visit over two days and stay in one of the on-site hotels. Legoland has an abundance of eateries, but by far the cheapest option is to bring your own picnic. There's plenty of retail temptation as well, including the Big Shop that's a veritable Aladdin's cave for Lego fans.

Food & Drink

• Like its rides, Legoland's eating options are very child friendly – from pizza and burgers to fish and chips, plus wraps, chicken, pasta and more. There are plenty of sweet temptations, too, from ice cream to waffles to sweets (10am-5pm, £).

Port Lympne

Food & Drink

- **Babydoll's Wood Fired Pizza:** On-site Italian restaurant set in landscaped gardens (01303-234181, noon-9pm, £).

- **Moroccan Courtyard:** Once the venue for high society parties, the hotel's authentic restored courtyard is now a charming restaurant for breakfast, lunch, afternoon tea and dinner (01303-234111, noon-9pm, £).

Address: Port Lympne, Aldington Road, Lympne, Hythe, Kent CT21 4LR (aspinallfoundation.org/port-lympne)

Rail: from 37min to Ashford International via St Pancras/Charing Cross stations, then Stagecoach bus 10/taxi (10mi)

Road: 1hr 40min (74mi) via A2 & M20

Opening Times: Apr-Oct 9.30am-6.30pm, Oct-Mar 9.30am-5pm (see website for dates)

Fees: £26 (child £17.60)

Nearby: Dymchurch, Folkestone, Hythe, Romney Marsh

Located close to the village of Lympne (near Hythe) in Kent (74 miles from London), Port Lympne is a wildlife park set in 600 acres, incorporating a historic mansion (now a hotel) and landscaped gardens designed by Sir Herbert Baker for Sir Philip Sassoon during the First World War. The estate was purchased in 1973 by John Aspinall, who was running out of space at his Howletts Wild Animal Park (near Canterbury), and has been open to the public since 1976. Since 1984 it has been owned by the John Aspinall Foundation, a world-class conservation charity dedicated to protecting endangered animals around the globe. Although Port Lympne is home to over 700 animals across 90 species, it isn't a zoo but rather a breeding sanctuary for rare and endangered species; where possible, captive bred animals are returned to protected wilderness areas and reserves worldwide. The reserve is also known for encouraging a close relationship between staff and animals.

Among the animals at Port Lympne is the largest breeding herd of black rhinoceros in the UK, plus Siberian tigers, western lowland gorillas, monkeys, Malayan tapirs, Barbary lions and African hunting dogs.

Hotel

Your safari adventure begins at basecamp, where you board a safari truck and journey out to 'South America, Asia and Africa' to view rhino, giraffe, zebra, deer and wildebeest. The South American experience is home to spectacled (Andean) bears, rhea, Brazilian tapir, capybara, coatimundi and vicuña, while in the African experience you'll encounter free roaming herds of Africa's most iconic wildlife. In Carnivore Territory you come face to face with majestic big cats and elusive small cats, while in the Asian experience you'll encounter wallowing water buffalo and herds of deer.

The reserve offers a number of dining options (see **Food & Drink** box) and you can stay overnight at the Port Lympne hotel, along with various lodges and glamping options. If you wish to stay longer there's lots to see and do in the surrounding area, including visiting beautiful 13th-century Lympne Castle, the historic coastal towns of Dymchurch and Hythe, and magnificent Romney Marsh.

Red Panda

African Painted Dogs

Chapman Zebras

Among the attractions at Port Lympne is the UK's largest Dinosaur Forest, where you'll meet tyrannosaurus rex, stegosaurus, pterodactyls and diplodocus. You can even make them come to life with the park's virtual reality app – if you dare! As you journey through three acres of natural woodland, you'll discover fascinating facts about the prehistoric world and can even become an amateur palaeontologist digging for fossils.

Giraffe & Safari Truck

RAF Museum London

Address: RAF Museum London, Grahame Park Way, NW9 5LL (rafmuseum.org.uk/london)

Rail: from 30min by Northern Line tube to Colindale via King's Cross station, then bus/walk (½mi)

Road: 40min (10mi) via A41

Opening Times: 10am-5/6pm (see website)

Fees: free admission, parking fee, flight simulators £3-£6, 4D theatre £5

Nearby: Elstree Studios, Harrow, Wembley

Flight Simulators

The museum offers a range of unique hands-on experiences (for a fee). Discover your inner aviator in a Pilot Zone Simulator, climb aboard the Eurofighter Typhoon Simulator or enjoy a 4D ride with the Red Arrows. The 4D Theatre combines cutting-edge 3D computer animation with the added dimension of dynamic seating and special effects, transporting you into the middle of the action to become the pilot of a B-17 Bomber over enemy territory, an ace pilot in the desert (ravine) race of your life, or a time traveller, fast-forwarding through the decades to witness the greatest advances of aviation technology.

Somewhat hidden away in an unfashionable north London suburb (just 10 miles from central London) on the site of a former aerodrome, the Royal Air Force (RAF) Museum is one of the world's best flight exhibits. Opened in 1972, it's the UK's only national museum devoted wholly to aviation – split between this site and RAF Cosford in Shropshire – with over 100 aircraft from around the world, from very early designs to current jets and military aircraft. The museum is housed in six huge buildings and covers aviation history from early balloon flights to the latest jet fighters. An upper floor allows visitors to overlook the hangars, while platforms allow you to get close to the aircraft.

The Aeronauts interactive centre has over 40 'hands on' experiments to help visitors understand how an aircraft flies, while in the Immersive Histories section you can join the Dambusters (age 13+, £10 fee) on their legendary mission or take the pilot's seat in one of Britain's greatest planes in the Spitfire Experience (£10). Three new innovative galleries in

hangar 1 explore the first 100 years of the RAF and its role today, while inviting visitors to imagine its future contribution and technology. Hangar 2 explores the First World War in the air, while hangars 3 to 6 depict aspects of aerial warfare from 1918 to 1980 and the RAF from 1980 to today. Aside from the permanent displays, there are special events, lectures and temporary exhibitions throughout the year.

The museum is vast and it's difficult to take in everything on one visit. With this in mind, the website has a useful facility that helps you make the best use of your time. And when you need to touch down for a break, there are a number of cafés (see **Food & Drink** box) and areas set aside for picnics.

Food & Drink

- **Sunderland & Wessex Cafés:** Located next to the Sunderland Flying Boat in hangars 1 and 3 respectively, these cafés are ideal for a light snack (Sunderland 10am-5pm, Wessex 11am-4pm, £).
- **Claude's Café:** Named after Claude Grahame-White, who founded London Aerodrome (the museum's site) in the early 1900s, Claude's Café offers everything from light snacks to hearty lunches (11am-4pm, £).

Spitfire

Tornado F3

Thorpe Park

> **Address:** Thorpe Park, Staines Rd, Chertsey, Surrey KT16 8PN (thorpepark.com)
>
> **Rail:** from 32min to Staines via Waterloo station, then 950 bus or taxi (3.4mi)
>
> **Road:** 50min (25mi) via M4
>
> **Opening Times:** 10am-4/8pm, depending on the time of year (see website)
>
> **Fees:** day tickets from £33 (see website)
>
> **Nearby:** Chessington, **Legoland**, **Painshill**, **RHS Wisley**, **Windsor**

A theme park located between Chertsey and Staines in Surrey (just 25 miles from London), Thorpe Park is home to over 30 rides, attractions and live events, mainly targeted at teenagers and young adults. It's targeted firmly at thrill seekers and horror movie buffs and has some of the more imaginative – and plain scary – rides, including Britain's fastest rollercoaster, Stealth.

Thorpe Park Resort was built in the '70s on a gravel pit – originally the site of the Thorpe Park Estate which was demolished some 40 years earlier – which was partially flooded to create a water-based theme for the park. The park was officially opened by Lord Louis Mountbatten in 1979

and has since grown into one of the UK's major theme parks. The first owners were Ready Mixed Concrete Limited, who sold it to the Tussauds Group in 1998. The site is operated by theme park specialists Merlin Entertainments who also manage Chessington World of Adventures (see page 154) and Legoland (see page 158).

> The downsides to Thorpe Park are the inevitable queues, limited staff and closed rides. It also has more than its fair share of 'wet' rides, so bring towels, swimwear and a change of clothes.

Major attractions include seven rollercoasters, including the Nemesis Inferno (see page 148), in which riders swing beneath the carriages; Stealth, which launches riders to 205ft at 80mph in just 2.5 seconds; Swarm, the UK's first winged rollercoaster; Saw - The Ride, the world's first horror movie themed coaster featuring a 100ft 'beyond-vertical' drop, and The Walking Dead, which drops zombies into the coaster thrill mix. Other flagship rides include the wet-knuckle experience of Tidal Wave, the gravity defying thrills of Zodiac, and Derren Brown's Ghost Train, which is advertised as a 'multi-sensory dark ride' and pulls no punches. More (young) child-friendly attractions include a seaside area called Amity Beach and an Angry Birds themed land.

Colossus

The park is split into eight main territories, to fit in with the 'island theme' of the park. Visitors begin at **Port and Basecamp**, and can then explore **Amity**, which opened with Tidal Wave and now includes Stealth, Amity Beach and Storm Surge; **The Jungle** containing Nemesis Inferno, Rumba Rapids and a street of restaurants; **Angry Birds' Land** where attractions include Angry Birds 4D, Detonator: Bombs Away (drop tower) and King Pig's Wild Hog Dodgems; the **Old Town** near the back of the park, including Saw - The Ride, Rocky Express and Lumber Jump; the **Lost City** containing Colossus, Vortex and Zodiac; **Swarm Island**, opened as the plaza for The Swarm; and the **Dock Yard**, where you'll find Derren Brown's Ghost Train and The Walking Dead.

Thorpe Park has a seemingly limitless number of places to eat, although picnics are permitted, and you can stay overnight at the Thorpe Shark Hotel, which you enter through the jaws of a great white shark.

Zodiac

Vortex

Food & Drink

• Thorpe Park offers the usual theme park fare with choices including Fin's Bar and Grill, Infernos Pizza and Pasta, and Amity Kebabs, plus the usual ice cream and donut temptations dotted around the park (10am-4/8pm, £).

Swarm

Woburn Safari Park

Address: Woburn Safari Park, Crawley Rd, Woburn, Bedford MK17 9QN (woburnsafari.co.uk)

Rail: only accessible by car

Road: 1hr 15min (49mi) via J13 of the M1

Opening Times: Mar-Oct 10am-6pm (see website for Feb/Nov dates and times)

Fees: £24.99 (child £17.99)

Nearby: Bletchley, Woburn Abbey, **ZSL Whipsnade Zoo**

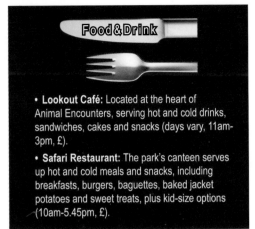

Food & Drink

• **Lookout Café:** Located at the heart of Animal Encounters, serving hot and cold drinks, sandwiches, cakes and snacks (days vary, 11am-3pm, £).

• **Safari Restaurant:** The park's canteen serves up hot and cold meals and snacks, including breakfasts, burgers, baguettes, baked jacket potatoes and sweet treats, plus kid-size options (10am-5.45pm, £).

Located in Woburn, Bedfordshire (49 miles from London), Woburn Safari Park is the UK's largest drive-through safari park. It's part of the Duke of Bedford's estate, which also includes Woburn Abbey and a 3,000-acre deer park. The safari park – created by the 13th Duke of Bedford on the grounds of Woburn Abbey – opened in 1970 to supplement the income of the estate and restore the Abbey, which had fallen into disrepair as a consequence of the Second World War and high post-war taxes. Today, Woburn is committed to animal conservation and is involved in international breeding programmes to help save endangered species.

The 360-acre park is home to over 1,000 animals, which roam freely while visitors drive through their enclosures. Species include southern white rhino, elands, scimitar-horned oryx, Ankole cattle, African wild asses, Asian elephants, Bactrian camels, bongo, Père David's deer, black bears and Barbary monkeys. The Road Safari's route takes you on an hour's drive through five areas, commencing in the Northern Plains with bison and zebra, followed by the Savannah Grasslands (rhino and

Feeding the Giraffes

wildebeest), Kingdom of the Carnivores (lions, tigers and Canadian timber wolves), Giraffe Junction (the largest herd in Europe) and African Forest (Barbary macaques).

The park also has a foot safari called A Walk on the Wild Side, which is home to many smaller animals including slender tailed meerkats, elephants, sea lions, African crested porcupine, four species of lemurs and many others. The Great Woburn Railway takes you on a gentle scenic tour of the foot safari area, stopping on hourly trips at the Alpaca Outpost where you can feed the alpaca herd. Animal Encounters is a 40-acre leisure area featuring animal talks, petting zones, a gift shop, family restaurant, a Go Ape zip-wire course and Giraffe Trail High Ropes. Animals here include lemurs, squirrel monkeys, wallabies, rheas, penguins, goats, ponies, reptiles, red pandas and marmosets. There's also a soft play centre called the Mammoth Play Ark and Swan and Dragon boats.

Woburn offers a number of cafés and restaurants (see **Food & Drink** box), or you can bring your own food and eat in one of the designated picnic areas.

Woburn Abbey

The adjacent Woburn Abbey & Gardens (see woburnabbey.co.uk) is well worth a visit, although it's only open in spring and summer and it isn't possible to combine the safari park with the abbey (it's physically impossible to see both in a day – you need an overnight stop). The abbey was founded by the Cistercians in 1145, and after being dissolved was given to John Russell, 1st Earl of Bedford, by Henry VIII in 1547. The handsome mansion was largely rebuilt in 1744 and contains one of the most important private art collections in the world, including works by Gainsborough, Hogarth, Lely, Rembrandt, Reynolds, Rubens, Tintoretto, Van Dyck and Velázquez, while the 28-acre Humphry Repton-inspired gardens are a delight.

Siberian (Amur) Tiger

Lion family

Southern White Rhino

ZSL Whipsnade Zoo

ℹ️

Address: ZSL Whipsnade Zoo, Whipsnade, Dunstable, Beds LU6 2LF (zsl.org/zsl-whipsnade-zoo).

Rail: from 31min to Luton via St Pancras station, then taxi (9mi)

Road: 1hr 15min (49mi) via M1

Opening Times: Mar-Aug 10am-5pm, Sep-Feb 10am-3/4pm (see website)

Fees: peak £29.25 (child £19.01) online, free external car park - see website for offers

Nearby: Bletchley, Chilterns, Luton, St Albans, Waddesdon, Woburn

Asian Elephants

Located near Dunstable in Bedfordshire, 49 miles from London, ZSL (Zoological Society of London) Whipsnade Zoo is one of two zoos owned by the ZSL; the other is ZSL London Zoo. The ZSL is a charity devoted to the worldwide conservation of animals and their habitats. It was founded in 1826 by Sir Stamford Raffles (1781-1826, founder of modern Singapore in 1819) with the aim of promoting the worldwide conservation of animals and their habitats. His dream became a reality when ZSL London Zoo opened in Regent's Park in 1828. A century later, ZSL secretary Sir Peter Chalmers Mitchell had the idea of creating a park zoo – similar to New York's Bronx Zoo – and the

ZSL purchased a derelict farm as the site for the new venture. When Whipsnade Park Zoo opened in 1931, it was the first open zoo in Europe that was easily accessible to visitors.

Whipsnade is the UK's largest zoo and one of Europe's largest wildlife conservation parks, home to over 200 species (3,800 animals) in a park extending to 600 acres. Due to its huge size, park visitors may use the zoo's bus service or drive their own cars between the various animal enclosures. The zoo also has a

In addition to the large outdoor exhibits, there's also an indoor exhibit housing a number of smaller, exotic animals such as snakes, spiders and chameleons, plus a butterfly house, children's farm and a brand-new aquarium (opened July 2019).

steam train service, the 762mm narrow gauge Great Whipsnade Railway, aka the Jumbo Express.

Today, Whipsnade Zoo is home to an abundance of animals that can be viewed in their huge outdoor enclosures, rather than in small cages. In Wild Wild Whipsnade you can see beasts that roamed wild in Britain hundreds of years ago, including brown bears, wolverines, Eurasian lynx, wild boar, European bison, moose and reindeer. Other major exhibits include Lions of the Serengeti (home to a pride of seven African lions), Passage through Asia (Bactrian camels, plus fallow, sika and Père David's deer), Rhinos of Nepal, the Chimpnasium, Cheetah Rock and Birds of the World.

Animal demonstrations, talks, shows and feeds take place daily, while you can take part in a number of 'experiences' (fee) such as becoming an elephant keeper or feeding the giraffes. There's no shortage of food for humans either, as Whipsnade offers a number of cafés and restaurants (see **Food & Drink** box), plus some tasty picnic spots.

Food & Drink

- **Base Camp Restaurant:** Offers tasty classics such as sausage and mash and 'proper' burgers in a comfortable, family-friendly setting (10am until 30m before closing, £).
- **River Cottage Kitchen & Deli:** Overlooking the white rhinos enclosure, this eatery follows Hugh Fearnley-Whittingstall's commitment to sustainably-sourced seasonal ingredients, and offers a kids' menu, too (10am until two hours before closing, £).

Cheetahs

Brown Bears

Ring Tailed Lemur

Stonehenge, Wiltshire (see page 184)

7.
Miscellaneous

This chapter contains suggestions for days out from London that don't fit conveniently into other chapters, such as the beautiful regions of the Chilterns and Cotswolds, absorbing Bletchley Park and prehistoric Stonehenge, historic Dorking (for its antiques shops) and lovely Surrey Hills, Mayfield Lavendar Farm and Ridgeview Vineyard, and the captivating Watts Gallery & Artists' Village in Surrey.

Most can be reached in less than 90 minutes by train (many in less than an hour), although if you wish to tour or combine a visit with other venues, then you're better off travelling by car.

Beaulieu & the New Forest

Address: Beaulieu, New Forest, Hampshire SO42 7ZN (beaulieu.co.uk)

Rail: from 1h 32min to Brockenhurst via Waterloo station, then taxi (7mi)

Road: 1h 55min (91mi) via M3 & M27 (junction 2)

Opening Times: 10am-5pm (6pm summer)

Fees: £24.75 (£19.50 online at least a day in advance), child £12.50 (£9.50)

Nearby: Buckler's Hard, Exbury Gardens, Lyndhurst, **Salisbury**, Southampton, **Winchester**

New Forest

A National Park since 2005, the New Forest is noted for its heathland, forest trails, native ponies and lovely villages; from magnificent scenery to free-roaming animals, fascinating history to scenic coastline, the park offers something for everyone.

Charming Beaulieu village – the name, pronounced 'Bewley', derives from the Latin *bellus locus regis*, meaning 'beautiful place of the king' – is situated on the edge of the New Forest National Park in Hampshire (91 miles from London), at the heart of the 7,000-acre Beaulieu estate. The estate is home to the National Motor Museum, Palace House, Beaulieu Abbey ruins and much more, and you can explore the attractions with unlimited rides on the 'Skytrain' monorail and a replica 1912 open-top bus.

Situated at the head of the picturesque Beaulieu River, the village dates back to the 13th century, when it grew up around the abbey founded in 1204 by Cistercian monks on land given to them by King John, who had a royal hunting lodge at Beaulieu. The king had quarrelled with the Cistercian order early in his reign and established the abbey to atone for his past oppressions.

Palace House, originally the 13th-century gatehouse of **Beaulieu Abbey**, has been the ancestral home of a branch of the Montagu family since 1538, when it was purchased from the crown by Sir Thomas Wriothesley (later 1st Earl of Southampton) following the Dissolution of the Monasteries by Henry VIII. The house was extended in the 16th century and again in the 19th century and today is a fine example of a Victorian Gothic country house; it's no longer home to Lord and Lady Montagu, who live in a modern villa on the estate. The house and its beautiful gardens are open to the public, while the tranquil abbey's remains

Beaulieu Palace House

are beautifully preserved and provide an oasis of calm. Among the surviving monastery buildings are the domus (once the lay brothers' living quarters, now containing a museum and hosting functions and exhibitions), and the monks' refectory, which became the **Beaulieu Parish Church** soon after the abbey was destroyed.

One of Beaulieu's main attractions is the **National Motor Museum** (opened in 1952 as the Montagu Motor Museum), which has a collection of over 250 iconic cars and motorcycles from the early days of the motor car through to the modern day. Exhibits include vehicles used to set world land-speed records and Formula 1 racing cars, while *Top Gear* fans will enjoy exploring the **World of Top Gear**, featuring vehicles that have appeared in the popular BBC series. Beaulieu also has a **Secret Army Exhibition** which tells the story of its role as a top-secret training establishment for special agents of the Special Operations Executive (SOE) during the Second World War.

Beaulieu hosts a comprehensive programme of motoring-related events throughout the year and in 2019 Beaulieu staged a unique exhibition of over 250 sculptures by national and international sculptors.

If you're tempted to stay over for a few days there's a wealth of interesting places to visit in the New Forest, including Exbury Gardens and steam railway, Buckler's Hard, Brockenhurst, Lyndhurst and the New Forest Wildlife Park, to name just a few.

Food & Drink

- **Brabazon Restaurant:** Beaulieu's on-site restaurant serves hot lunches with an emphasis on fresh local produce and includes a children's menu (lunch 11.30am-2.30pm, £).

- **Coffee Shop:** On-site coffee shop serving sandwiches, baguettes, toasties and delicious homemade cakes and pastries (10am-6pm, £).

Beaulieu Abbey

New Forest Ponies

Beaulieu Village

Bletchley Park

Address: The Mansion, Bletchley Park, Sherwood Drive, Bletchley, Milton Keynes, Bucks MK3 6EB (bletchleypark.org.uk)

Rail: from 33min via Euston station

Road: 1h 25min (51mi) via M1 & A5

Opening Times: Mar-Oct 9.30am-5pm, Nov-Feb 9.30am-4pm

Fees: £20 (child 12-17 £12, under-12s free)

Nearby: Chilterns, St Albans, Waddesdon, ZSL Whipsnade Zoo, Woburn Safari Park

Food & Drink

• **Hut 4 Café:** Tuck into soups, salads, jacket spuds and hot dishes in the former WW2 Naval Intelligence Codebreaking Hut, with children's lunch boxes available (9.30am-4/5pm, £).

• **Three Trees:** Large, upscale pub in Bletchley with a beer garden, serving modern British food and featuring a superb carvery (01908-366816, noon-8/9pm, £).

A 19th-century mansion and estate in Bletchley, Buckinghamshire, 51 miles from London, Bletchley Park is celebrated as the main site for British (and subsequently Allied) codebreaking during the Second World War. At the time of its operation it was a closely guarded secret and only 30 years later was the vital contribution to the war effort by codebreakers such as Alan Turing fully understood. The team at Bletchley Park devised automatic machinery to help with decryption, culminating in the development of Colossus, the world's first programmable digital electronic computer. Codebreaking operations at Bletchley Park ended in 1946 and all information about the wartime operations was classified until the mid-'70s. The historical importance of Bletchley cannot be over-estimated: according to the official historian of British Intelligence, the 'Ultra' intelligence (the ultimate level of secrecy) discovered there shortened the war by two to four years and without it, the outcome would have been uncertain.

The site appears in the *Domesday Book* of 1086 as part of the manor of Eaton and it only became known as Bletchley Park in the 1870s. The 581-acre Bletchley estate was purchased in 1883 by financier and politician Sir Herbert Samuel Leon, who expanded the existing farmhouse into the mansion you see today, an ill-assorted mixture of Victorian Gothic, Tudor and Dutch Baroque styles. In May 1938, Admiral Sir Hugh Sinclair – head of the Secret Intelligence Service (SIS or

Bletchley Park Mansion

MI6) – purchased the mansion and 58 acres of land for £6,000 for use by the SIS in the event of war. He used his own money as the government claimed not to have sufficient funds!

The Enigma Machine

The most common method employed by the Germans to transmit secret messages during the Second World War was via the Enigma machine, an encryption device developed in the early- to mid-20th century. They thought its code was impenetrable and it was – until one of the devices was captured by the Allies in May 1941 from a German U-boat. Its cipher keys and code books allowed Bletchley codebreakers to read German Enigma-encrypted signal traffic throughout the war.

Bletchley Park – and its famous huts where the codebreakers worked – was saved from developers in 1991 when the Bletchley Park Trust was formed. Opened to the public in 1994, it houses interpretive exhibits and huts rebuilt as they were during wartime operations, including Hut 8 which features Alan Turing's office, recreated to how it would have looked during the war, complete with his mug chained to the radiator. Block H is home to the **National Museum of Computing**, opened in 2007. Here the Colossus (which includes a rebuilt Colossus machine) and Tunny galleries tell the story of the Allies' wartime codebreaking, while the

museum also charts the development of computing from the mainframes of the '60s and '70s to the rise of personal computing in the '80s.

Today, Bletchley Park is an internationally renowned heritage attraction, welcoming visitors from around the world, celebrating Britain's wartime successes and those who helped make them happen.

Hut 4

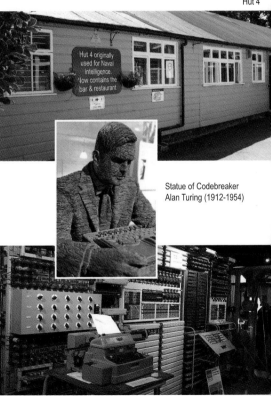

Statue of Codebreaker Alan Turing (1912-1954)

National Museum of Computing

The Chilterns

Suggested base: Amersham, Bucks HP7 0DG
(chilternsaonb.org, visitchilterns.co.uk)

Rail: from 31min via Marylebone station or
Metropolitan Line tube (ca 50m)

Road: 59min (28mi) via A40 & A413

Nearby: Bekonscot, Chenies Manor, **Cookham,
Great Missenden,** High Wycombe, **Oxford, St
Albans**

The Chilterns – officially called the Chiltern Hills – is a range of rolling peaks northwest of London, extending across Oxfordshire, Buckinghamshire, Hertfordshire and Bedfordshire. They cover 322mi², stretching 45 miles southwest to northeast from Goring-on-Thames (Oxfordshire) to Hitchin (Hertfordshire), much of which has been designated an Area of Outstanding Natural Beauty (AONB) since 1965.

Quintessential English countryside, the Chilterns contains some of the finest landscapes in Britain. More than 20 per cent of it is wooded, while two-thirds is given over to agriculture, and its character has been shaped by its inhabitants for centuries, from the rolling fields to the picturesque villages and hamlets. The Chilterns rest on a chalk escarpment and this has created a unique environment. The velvety chalk downs are rich in herbs, flowers and grasses – some of which are unique to the area – while springs emerge to feed clear, sparkling chalk streams, such as the Chess and Misbourne. One of the Chilterns' most delightful rivers, the Misbourne rises above Great Missenden and flows for 17 miles via Amersham and the Chalfonts to Denham, where it meets the River Colne and, eventually, the Thames.

In an area as large as the Chilterns it's difficult to pick one town as a base for a day trip, but we've settled on historic **Amersham**, one of the Chilterns' loveliest market towns. With a history dating back to Anglo-Saxon times, Amersham is made up of two distinct areas: Old Amersham, set in the valley of the River Misbourne, which contains the 13th-century parish church of **St Mary's** and several historic pubs and coaching inns; and its modern counterpart, Amersham-on-the-Hill, which grew up around the railway station following the

---

Amersham has appeared in a number of films, not least the 1994 rom com *Four Weddings and a Funeral.* **The King's Arms** (see **Food & Drink**) stood in for The Lucky Boatman, where Andie MacDowell and Hugh Grant got together after the first wedding, although the four-poster room they stayed in is actually just along the High Street in **The Crown Hotel**.

arrival of the Metropolitan Railway in 1892. The broad High Street, with its half-timbered houses, cottages and handsome Market House, makes Amersham one of the most popular of the Chiltern valley towns, with a wide choice of restaurants, pubs and independent shops. Its fascinating history is told in the **Amersham Museum**, located in a Tudor building in Old Amersham High Street. Guided walks of the Old Town depart from the museum on selected days (see amershammuseum.org/events/guided-walks).

If you want to explore further afield, there are three pretty circular walks in the Misbourne Valley that you can enjoy from Amersham; a free leaflet can be downloaded from the Chilterns AONB website (www.chilternsaonb.org/uploads/files/walks_and_rides/misbournewalks.pdf). Four miles east of Amersham is spectacular **Chenies Manor House**, one of the UK's finest Tudor mansions (Apr-Oct, Wed-Thu 2-5pm, fee) with a beautiful garden.

If you're tempted to stay longer, there are good hotels and restaurants throughout the region – and at just half an hour from London by train, it's easy to return.

Food & Drink

• **King's Arms Hotel:** Beautiful 15th-century inn with 35 rooms in Amersham, with a delightful restaurant in which to enjoy lunch (01494-725722, lunch noon-2.30pm, Sat-Sun noon-9.30/8pm, £-££).

• **Seasons Café Deli:** Relaxed licensed café in Old Amersham serving good coffee and a menu of all-time favourites, plus tapas on Thursday nights (01494-728070, 7/8am-5/6pm, 10pm Thu, £).

King's Arms Hotel

Chenies Manor House

The Cotswolds

Suggested base: Moreton-in-Marsh, Gloucestershire GL56 0AA (cotswolds.com, cotswoldsaonb.org.uk)

Rail: from 1h 33min to Moreton-in-Marsh via Paddington station

Road: 2h (88mi) via M40 & A44

Nearby: Broadway, Chipping Campden, Chipping Norton, Stow-on-the-Wold

Food & Drink

• **Black Bear Inn:** Located on the High Street (Moreton), this friendly pub serves good food from local suppliers washed down with local ales (01608-652992, lunch noon-2.30pm, £).

• **Cotswold Tearoom:** Cosy licensed tearoom in Moreton with a beautiful walled garden, serving breakfasts, lunches and the quintessential cream tea (9am-5pm, 4pm Sun, £).

The glorious sweep of the Cotswold Hills begins in the meadows of the upper Thames and rises to an escarpment known as the Cotswold Edge, just southeast of the Severn Valley and Evesham Vale. Designated an Area of Outstanding Natural Beauty (AONB) in 1966 – the largest in the UK – the Cotswolds cover an area of 787mi^2, some 25 miles wide and 90 miles long, which stretches southwest from Stratford-upon-Avon (Warks) to Bath (Somerset), contained mostly within Gloucestershire and Oxfordshire.

One of the loveliest regions in the UK, the Cotswolds are noted for their rural charm, lush countryside, idyllic picture-postcard villages and vibrant market towns. These ancient landscapes are crisscrossed by some 4,000 miles of historic stone walls – a legacy of the wool trade that boosted the area's wealth in the Middle Ages – and characterised by houses built from the local honey-coloured limestone. Today's Cotswolds are home to royals, celebrities and some of the most sought-after addresses in the UK. They captivate film makers and authors – they're the inspiration for Jilly Cooper's *Rutshire Chronicles* – and, of course, tourists, who descend in their thousands every day.

The Cotswolds are the perfect place for walking, cycling, riding or simply relaxing. There's a chocolate-box assortment of attractive towns and villages – from Broadway and Bourton-on-the-Water to Chipping Campden and Stow-on-the-Wold – and it's hard to know which to choose. But we have settled on the market

Chipping Campden

town of **Moreton-in-Marsh**, around 90 minutes from London by direct train.

In the centre of Moreton-in-Marsh is Redesdale Hall. Erected in 1887 by Sir Algernon Bertram Freeman Mitford, 1st Baron Redesdale – Lord of the Manor of Moreton and paternal grandfather of the infamous Mitford sisters – it's now home to crafts fairs and council meetings.

A thriving market town in the beautiful Evenlode Valley – at the crossroads of the Roman Fosse Way (now the A429) and the A44 – Moreton's history stretches back over 1,000 years. On Tuesdays it hosts the largest street market in the Cotswolds (it has had a market charter since 1226). The broad High Street is lined with elegant 17th- and 18th-century buildings hewn from Cotswold stone, among them the **White Hart Royal Hotel**, a former manor house where Charles I sheltered during the Civil War (a copy of the King's unpaid bill is displayed on a plaque in the entrance lobby) and the rare 16th-century **Curfew Tower** with its original clock and bell. Nearby attractions include Batsford Arboretum, the Cotswold Falconry Centre, Bourton House Garden and Sezincote Gardens, all of which are accessible from Moreton via local footpaths.

Wherever you are in the Cotswolds you're never more than a few steps away from unspoilt countryside – with over 3,000 miles of footpaths and bridleways, including the 102-mile Cotswold Way, which leads northeast from Bath to Chipping Camden. And if you can't tear yourself away, there's a profusion of enchanting hotels and excellent restaurants, along with an annual programme of carnivals, fairs and festivals.

Moreton Market

Broadway

Moreton-in-Marsh in autumn

Dorking & the Surrey Hills

Address: Dorking, Surrey RH4 1TF (visitdorking.com, surreyhills.org).

Rail: from 49min via Waterloo station

Road: 1h 10min (27mi) via A3

Nearby: Box Hill, Guildford, **Polesden Lacey**, **Shere**, Surrey Hills AONB

A historic market town in Surrey, 27 miles south of London, Dorking is well known for its range of independent shops – antiques and crafts a speciality – and its glorious location in the heart of the Surrey Hills, an Area of Outstanding Natural Beauty (AONB), just west of the Vale of Holmsdale at the foot of the North Downs. The town is bisected by Pipp Brook (and mill pond), a tributary of the River Mole which flows north from here to the River Thames.

Dorking's history dates back to the Romans – Stane Street, the Roman road between London and Chichester, passed through the town – although the name comes from the Saxon *Dorchinges*. By the time of the *Domesday Book* (1086) the Manor of Dorking covered the modern parishes of Dorking, Capel and the Holmwoods. The town later became a prosperous agricultural and market town, capitalising on its position at the junction of a number of long-distance roads.

> The countryside around Dorking has some of the UK's finest hiking paths, including the Deepdene Trail, Greensand Way, the Mole Gap Trail, the Pilgrims Way and the North Downs Way.

Today, Dorking is a thriving market town with an eclectic mix of architectural styles, including some buildings dating back to the 14th century, although much of the architecture is Victorian and Edwardian, reflecting its growth following the opening of the rail line to London in 1867 (the town now has three railway stations!). You can follow the heritage trail around the town (visitdorking.com/content/files/2017/05/heritage-front.pdf) and discover the town's history at **Dorking Museum** (Thu-Sat 10am-4pm), which provides a 21st century interactive experience. One of the town's most prominent landmarks is splendid Art Deco **Dorking Halls**, the Mole Valley's leading entertainment venue,

Dorking from Box Hill

Food & Drink

- **Mullins Coffee Shop:** Located on West Street in the ancestral home of William Mullins, one of the Pilgrim Fathers, Mullins serves breakfast, lunch and afternoon tea with some truly scrumptious cakes (9.30am-4/4.30pm, Sun 10am-3pm, closed Mon, £).

- **King's Arms:** Built in 1405 and named for Charles II (who allegedly stayed here), the King's Arms offers fine ales and food (01306-886496, noon-11pm/midnight, £).

home to a three-screen cinema, drama, opera and ballet performances, plus a café-bar. It's also the venue for exhibitions and fairs, including regular antiques fairs.

Antiques are one of the main reasons we've included Dorking in this chapter. The renowned **antiques quarter** is centred on West Street – the oldest part of town – and is home to an abundance of antiques and vintage shops, alongside purveyors of arts and crafts, smart boutiques, contemporary art galleries, jewellers, interior specialists and florists. If shopping is your passion, Dorking also has a 700-year-old **Market**, held in St Martin's car park on Fridays (8.30am-3pm).

The other reason for heading to Dorking is its enviable position in the beautiful Surrey Hills. **Box Hill** – Britain's first country park managed by the National Trust – is just three miles north of the town on the east bank of the Mole, while on the west bank is **Denbies**, the UK's

largest vineyard. To the north is glorious **Norbury Park**, which contains the Druids Grove, a forest of ancient yew trees, while to the southwest is **Leith Hill**, also owned by the NT. Leith Hill is the second-highest point in southeast England after Walbury Hill in Berkshire, and its tower stands around 1,000ft above sea level. From the top on a clear day it's said you can see the English Channel and Big Ben (Palace of Westminster).

Stepping Stones, River Mole

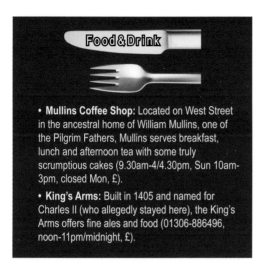

West Street

Deepdene Trail

Mayfield Lavender Farm

Food & Drink

- **Mayfield Farm Café:** The licensed café offers everything from hot drinks and light lunches to a lavender cream tea and even lavender cider (9am-6pm, £).

Address: Mayfield Lavender Farm, 1 Carshalton Road, Banstead, Surrey SM7 3JA (mayfieldlavender.com)

Rail: from 20min to West Croydon via London Bridge, Blackfriars or Victoria stations, then 166 bus (4mi)

Road: 1h (15mi) via A23

Opening Times: 1st June to mid-September, 9am-6pm (see website)

Fees: £2.50 (child under 16 free)

Nearby: Chessington, Dorking, Polesden Lacey, Surrey Hills AONB

Located 15 miles south of London, Mayfield Lavender Farm in Woodmansterne, Surrey, is a must-see during high summer, when you can wander through a sea of aromatic, organic lavender. The 25-acre farm was created by Brendan Maye, originally the MD of Wella who owned the Yardley Old English Lavender brand. In 2002 Maye secured the lease of a former Victorian lavender field in partnership with a local environmental charity, and together with his wife Lorna began growing the fragrant crop.

The farm has been open to visitors since 2008 and attracts thousands of people each year. It grows three different varieties of lavender, which usually start to bloom towards the end of June, with the peak in July and August – the weather can influence this so check the website before you visit. You can take a tractor ride (£2) around the farm; an effortless way to experience the undulating purple expanse of lavender and a plethora of happy bees and butterflies. Sadly, you cannot picnic among the blooms, although the café is worth a visit.

The farm is only open in summer but there's a 12-acre nursery and gift shop in Epsom (open year-round) with a beautiful orchard containing over 500 plum and apple trees.

The business nearly failed in its first year when, having planted half the field with 70,000 tiny plugs, crows and magpies pulled up each and every one!

Ridgeview Vineyard & Winery

• **The Bull:** Voted Best Freehouse Pub of the Year 2018 (greatbritishpubawards.co.uk), this 16th-century inn in Ditchling serves delicious modern British cuisine (01273-843147, lunch noon-2.30pm, Sat-Sun noon-9/9.30pm, £-££).

Address: Ridgeview Vineyard & Winery, Fragbarrow Lane, Ditchling Common, West Sussex BN6 8TP (ridgeview.co.uk)

Rail: from 51min to Burgess Hill via Victoria station, then taxi (2mi)

Road: 1h 45min (48mi) via M23

Opening Times: daily 11am-4pm (but check)

Fees: complimentary tastings (no booking), pre-booked tour and tastings £20

Nearby: Brighton, Burgess Hill, Haywards Heath, Lewes, South Downs National Park

Producing quality sparkling wine since 1995, Ridgeview Vineyard & Winery is situated at the foot of the beautiful South Downs near the picturesque village of Ditchling in West Sussex (48 miles from London). One of the pioneers of English sparkling wine production, Ridgeview was founded by Mike and Chris Roberts, who – after much research – decided that the South Downs were ideal for the production of traditional method sparkling wine made from the three classic grape varieties: Chardonnay, Pinot Noir and Pinot Meunier.

Today, some 25 years later with the family's second-generation of winemakers at the helm –Tamara Roberts is CEO, her brother Simon head winemaker – Ridgeview produces over 250,000 bottles of sparkling wine annually. It's sold throughout the world and served at top tables, from Buckingham Palace's state banquets to 10 Downing Street.

Ridgeview is open daily for tastings and sales, and you can take a tour (group or private) of the state-of-the-art winery, while in summer you can book a hamper of goodies (see website) to enjoy in the glorious wine garden.

The winery has celebrated some remarkable accomplishments including winning the prestigious trophy for 'Best Sparkling Wine in the World 2010' at the *Decanter* World Wine Awards.

Stonehenge

Address: Stonehenge, near Amesbury, Wiltshire SP4 7DE (english-heritage.org.uk/visit/places/stonehenge)

Rail: from 1h 23min to Salisbury via Waterloo station, then bus/taxi (9mi)

Road: 1h 40min (86mi) via M3 & A303

Opening Times: Apr-Sep 9.30am-7/8pm, Oct-Mar closes 5pm

Fees: £21.10 (£12.70)

Nearby: Andover, **Salisbury**, Warminster

An unmistakeable silhouette on the skyline two miles west of Amesbury in Wiltshire (86 miles from London), Stonehenge is one of the UK's most famous landmarks, a legally protected ancient monument since 1882 and a UNESCO World Heritage Site (together with Avebury's stone circle, some 20 miles to the north) since 1986. The site is managed by English Heritage, while the surrounding land is owned by the National Trust. The world's most famous prehistoric monument, it consists of a ring of 43 standing stones – it's believed there were originally around 80 – each weighing between two and four tons, while some of the largest stones soar to 30 feet and weigh an estimated 25 tons. The stones are set within earthworks in the middle of the densest complex of Neolithic and Bronze Age monuments in England, including several hundred burial mounds.

In 1915, Stonehenge was purchased at auction – the first and only time it was ever offered for sale – for £6,600 by local resident Sir Cecil Chubb, who gave it to the nation in 1918 on the condition that the entrance fee was never more than a shilling (5p today) and was free to local residents. Nowadays it costs over £20 to visit the site, but locals are still entitled to free admission.

Archaeologists believe Stonehenge was constructed between 3000 and 2000BC, while the surrounding circular earth bank and ditch, which constitutes the earliest phase of the monument, has been dated to around 3100BC. Two kinds of stone are used at Stonehenge – the larger sarsens and the smaller 'bluestones'. Radiocarbon dating suggests that the first bluestones were raised between 2400 and 2200BC, although they may have been at the site as early as 3000BC. The sarsens were erected in two concentric

arrangements – an inner horseshoe and an outer circle – and the bluestones were set up between them in a double arc. The majority of the stones are thought to have come from the Preseli Hills in South Wales, some 150 miles away, either through glaciation or human transportation.

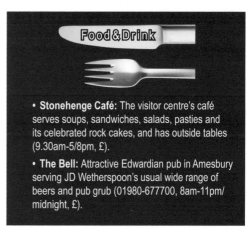

Food & Drink

• **Stonehenge Café:** The visitor centre's café serves soups, sandwiches, salads, pasties and its celebrated rock cakes, and has outside tables (9.30am-5/8pm, £).

• **The Bell:** Attractive Edwardian pub in Amesbury serving JD Wetherspoon's usual wide range of beers and pub grub (01980-677700, 8am-11pm/midnight, £).

Stonehenge may have served as a burial site, meeting place, solar calendar or sacred ritual, but it wasn't built (as some believe) as a druid temple. Druids, a group of Celtic pagans, have long used Stonehenge as a place of worship, although scholars believe it predates them by some 2,000 years. Nevertheless, each year hundreds of modern-day druids visit Stonehenge to mark the summer solstice (around 20th-22nd June).

You can no longer walk among the stones or touch them – to protect them from erosion – and they must be viewed from walkways. However, the nearby visitor centre features an interactive presentation that allows you to 'sit' among the stones as the

seasons change, while the site contains authentic replica Neolithic houses illustrating the tools and objects of everyday life. There's also an exhibition that tells the story of Stonehenge – the stones, the landscape, the people (including a reconstructed 5,500 year-old man) and its meaning – through a combination of audio-visual exhibits and over 250 archaeological objects and treasures discovered at the site.

Summer Solstice

Watts Gallery & Artists' Village

Address: Watts Gallery & Artists' Village, Down Lane, Compton, Surrey GU3 1DQ (wattsgallery.org.uk)

Rail: from 33min to Guildford via Waterloo station, then 46 bus/taxi (3mi)

Road: 1h 5min (35mi) via M25 & A3

Opening Times: Tue-Sun 10.30am-4/5pm, closed Mon

Fees: £11.50 (under 18s free, under 25s £5.75)

Nearby: Dorking, Godalming, Guildford, **Leonardslee Gardens**, **RHS Wisley**, **The Sculpture Park**, Surrey Hills AONB

Food & Drink

• **Tea Shop:** The gallery's café offers the usual cakes and cream teas, plus a selection of soups, sandwiches, salads and daily specials, and is noted for its Welsh rarebit (10.30am-4/5pm, £).

• **The Withies Inn:** 16th-century, wood-panelled freehouse in Compton with a cosy bar, first-class restaurant and nice garden (11am-11pm, Sun noon-4pm, £-££).

A hidden treasure secreted away in the village of Compton near Guildford (Surrey), 35 miles south of London, the Watts Gallery & Artists' Village is dedicated to the work of Victorian painter and sculptor George Frederic Watts (1817-1904), one of the most important artists and philanthropists of the 19th century. Watts holds a unique position within British art, as he found critical acclaim in his own lifetime – he was admired by fellow artists but also adored by the public – allowing him the platform to explore his idea of a poet-painter who could preach eternal truths and provoke social reform.

A portraitist, sculptor, landscape painter and symbolist, Watts' work embodied the most pressing ideas of the time, earning him the title of 'England's Michelangelo'. He was the creator of *Physical Energy*, an equestrian bronze that stands in London's Kensington Gardens, and the *Memorial to Heroic Self-Sacrifice* in

Limnerslease

London's Postman's Park, which commemorates brave acts by ordinary people. The Watts Gallery, founded in 1904, is a unique Arts and Crafts gem and one of a select group of galleries devoted to a single artist. The main exhibition features over 100 of Watts' works, spanning a period of 70 years, including portraits, landscapes and major symbolic works.

De Morgan Collection

Following the closure of the De Morgan Centre in London in 2014, the Watts Gallery has been home to the fabulous De Morgan Collection (see demorgan. org.uk) of works by William de Morgan (1839-1917) and his wife Evelyn (1855-1919). Key works from the collection are displayed in the Richard Jeffries Gallery in the main gallery building.

Watts had a strong artistic partnership with his second wife Mary (née Fraser Tytler, 1849-1938) who was a renowned designer in her own right, founder of the Compton Pottery (1900) and creator of the Watts Chapel. You can discover more about the couple in the Watts Studios, located in the restored east wing of their home, Limnerslease, and admire the exquisite Grade I listed Watts Chapel, an Arts and Crafts masterpiece designed and decorated by Mary and consecrated in 1898 (and still a working parish chapel). There are also some lovely woodlands and grounds to explore.

Today, the Artists' Village continues the Watts' legacy of 'Art for All', with its contemporary gallery (housed in the original pottery building), programme of temporary exhibitions, working artist in residence, conservation studios and extensive learning programme. You can purchase artwork from the contemporary exhibition, along with a wide range of gifts, books and homewares in the shop – and enjoy a break in the tea shop.

Main Exhibition

Watts Chapel

De Morgan Collection

London's Architectural Walks, 2nd edition

ISBN: 978-1-913171-01-8, 128 pages, softback, £9.99, Jim Watson

London's Architectural Walks is a unique guide to the most celebrated landmark buildings in one of the world's major cities. In thirteen easy walks, it takes you on a fascinating journey through London's diverse architectural heritage with historical background and clear maps. Some of the capital's most beautiful parks are visited, plus palaces, theatres, museums and some surprising oddities. The author's line and watercolour illustrations of all the city's significant buildings, make London's Architectural Walks an essential companion for anyone interested in the architecture that has shaped this great metropolis.

London's Secret Walks, 3rd edition

ISBN: 978-1-909282-99-5, 320 pages, softback, £10.99, Graeme Chesters

London is a great city for walking – whether for pleasure, exercise or simply to get from A to B. Despite the city's extensive public transport system, walking is often the quickest and most enjoyable way to get around – at least in the centre – and it's also free and healthy! Many attractions are off the beaten track, away from the major thoroughfares and public transport hubs. This favours walking as the best way to explore them, as does the fact that London is a visually interesting city with a wealth of stimulating sights in every 'nook and cranny'.

Touring the Cotswolds

ISBN: 978-1-909282-91-9, 128 pages, softback, £9.99, Jim Watson

Touring the Cotswolds is a unique guide to exploring the best of the Cotswolds by car through eight carefully planned tours, taking in the heavyweight tourist centres plus a wealth of hidden gems (the 'real Cotswolds'). You'll negotiate a maze of country lanes, high hills with panoramic views, lush woodlands and beautiful valleys, plus an abundance of picturesque villages, providing a comprehensive portrait of this varied and delightful area.

see citybooks.co

INDEX

London's Green Walks

ISBN: 978-1-909282-82-7, 192 pages, £9.99, David Hampshire

Green spaces cover almost 40 per cent of Greater London, ranging from magnificent royal parks and garden cemeteries, full of intrigue and history, to majestic ancient forests and barely tamed heathland; from elegant squares and formal country parks to enchanting 'secret' gardens. The 20 walks take in famous destinations, such as Hyde Park and Regent's Park, but also many smaller and lesser known – but no less beautiful – parks and gardens, all of which are free to explore.

London's Village Walks

ISBN: 978-1-909282-94-0, 192 pages, £9.99, David Hampshire

From its beginnings as a Roman trading port some 2,000 years ago, London has mushroomed into the metropolis we see today, swallowing up thousands of villages, hamlets and settlements in the process. Nevertheless, if you're seeking a village vibe you can still find it if you know where to look. Scratch beneath the surface of modern London and you'll find a rich tapestry of ancient villages just waiting to be rediscovered.

London's Monumental Walks

ISBN: 978-1-909282-95-7, 192 pages, £9.99, David Hampshire

It isn't perhaps surprising that in a city as rich in history as London, there's a wealth of public monuments, statues and memorials: in fact London probably has more statues than any other world city. Its streets, squares, parks and gardens are crammed with monuments to kings and queens, military heroes, politicians and local worthies, artists and writers, and notables from every walk of life (plus a few that commemorate deeds and people perhaps best forgotten), along with a wealth of abstract and contemporary works of art.

see citybooks.co

London's Waterside Walks

ISBN: 978-1-909282-96-4, 192 pages, softback, £9.99
David Hampshire

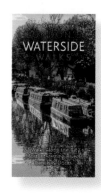

Most people are familiar with London's River Thames, but the city has much more to offer when it comes to waterways, including a wealth of canals, minor rivers (most are tributaries of the Thames), former docklands, lakes and reservoirs. *London's Waterside Walks* takes you along many of the city's lesser-known, hidden waterways.

Peaceful London, 2nd edition

ISBN: 978-1-909282-84-1, 192 pages, softback, £9.99
David Hampshire

Whether you're seeking somewhere to recharge your batteries, rest your head, revive your spirits, restock your larder or refuel your body; a haven to inspire, soothe or uplift your mood; or you just wish to discover a part of London that's a few steps further off the beaten track, *Peaceful London* will steer you in the right direction.

Quirky London, 2nd edition

ISBN: 978-1-990282-98-8, 208 pages, softback, £9.99
Graeme Chesters

London is a city with a cornucopia of strange sights and stories, being ancient, vast and in a constant state of flux. Unlike most guide books, *Quirky London* takes you off the beaten path to seek out the more unusual places and tales that fail to register on the radar of both visitors and residents alike, while also highlighting unusual and often overlooked aspects and attractions of some of London's most famous tourist sites.